MADISON

MADISON

HISTORY OF A MODEL CITY

ERIKA JANIK

THE History PRESS

Published by The History Press
Charleston, SC 29403
www.historypress.net

Front cover, top: State Street, 1939. *Wisconsin Historical Society Image #3151. Bottom*: German-American wurst roast. *Wisconsin Historical Society Image #1971.*

Back cover, top: Lakeside House. *Wisconsin Historical Society Image #25114. Bottom*: Mansion Hill Inn (formerly the Pierce House). *Image by author.*

First published 2010

Manufactured in the United States

ISBN 978.1.59629.121.8

Library of Congress Cataloging-in-Publication Data

Janik, Erika.
Madison : history of a model city / Erika Janik.
p. cm.
Includes bibliographical references.
ISBN 978-1-59629-121-8
1. Madison (Wis.)--History. 2. Madison (Wis.)--Social conditions. I. Title.
F589.M157J36 2010
977.5'83--dc22
2010033159

CONTENTS

ACKNOWLEDGEMENTS

While writing itself is a solitary pursuit, the process of putting together a book is certainly not. Thanks to the Wisconsin Historical Society for its tremendous historical riches and resources, both human and archival. Thanks, too, to the many historians, authors, residents, journalists, leaders and others who cared enough about Madison's future to leave a rich and colorful record of its past. Any errors or omissions are mine.

My friends put up with me for months as I worked on this book, offering encouragement, support and long lunch breaks. Thank you for still wanting to be my friends. My parents helped me move to Madison many years ago and have waited patiently for my return to Redmond, Washington. I'm sorry to tell you I'm still here, and now I've written a book about it. Thank you for understanding. Finally, and most especially, thanks to my husband, Matt, for his patience, good humor and generosity in listening to me talk history far more than any one person should have to bear. His constant support sees me through.

INTRODUCTION

Ebenezer Brigham left the first account of the land that would become Madison. Recalling his visit in 1828, he said, "The site was at the time an open prairie, on which grew dwarf oaks, while thickets covered the lower grounds." He then predicted, with remarkable foresight, that the land might be perfect for the capital of a new state (Wisconsin belonged to the Michigan Territory at the time).

Oddly enough, Jefferson Davis also passed through Madison in 1829. The future president of the Confederate States of America had been sent to Wisconsin to help build Fort Winnebago in 1828. Davis and his company of soldiers passed through Madison looking for deserters. He later recalled the area as abundant in fish and waterfowl and noted that the Indians ate primarily corn and wild rice.

Madison's beauty and potential were not obvious to all early visitors, however. To the soldiers pursuing Black Hawk in the summer of 1832, Madison did not leave a good impression. "If these lakes were anywhere else except in the country they are," wrote one, "they would be considered among the wonders of the world. But the country they are situated in, is not fit for any civilized nation of people to inhabit."

Fortunately, the man who would play an integral role in Madison's future took the former view when he first saw the isthmus in May 1829. Judge James Duane Doty, traveling overland from Green Bay to Prairie du Chien, liked what he saw so much that he purchased the land and platted a grid of streets for a future capital city that he called Madison. He then successfully lobbied the legislature for its creation.

Less than a century later, landscape architect John Nolen would show Madison an aspirational vision of itself that would serve as a challenge for future generations. His 1911 report revealed a Madison that took full advantage of its natural assets, a place as pleasing to the eye as it was to live and work. With just a little effort, Nolen said, Madison could become a model city for the world.

From its very beginning, Madison's story is one of its residents striving to achieve its potential, to become the world-class city that many people believed in and desperately wanted it to be. Farsighted leaders like James Doty, Lucius Fairchild, John Olin and John Nolen played integral roles in molding and forming the Madison of today.

Surrounded by lakes and located on an isthmus, water and land have played an integral part in Madison's past and present. The land and its resources have allowed people to survive and thrive here for thousands of years, creating an inseparable bond between natural and human histories.

Madison's story, while unique, is also part of a larger American story of settlement, growth, immigration and change. The city's history reflects all that has happened here, from glacial retreats and Ho-Chunk villages to city parks, Earth Day marches and the rich intellectual legacy of the University of Wisconsin. This book attempts to tell that story for residents both new and old.

1

ANCIENT PEOPLES

The Ho-Chunk called them *Tay-cho-per-ah*, or "Four Lakes." An 1832 American surveyor followed suit, labeling Madison's lakes numbers one through four. And so the lakes remained numerically named until 1854, when they finally received individual names—though Madison retains its "Four Lakes" nickname even today.

Water both defined and constrained Madison. Set on a narrow isthmus between Lakes Mendota and Monona, Madison is surrounded by a network of lakes, marshes, streams and rivers—a visible marker of the region's glacial past.

Only fifteen thousand years ago, most of North America lay beneath colossal sheets of ice. These advancing and retreating glaciers formed the headlands of Cape Cod and the Finger Lakes in upstate New York. But nowhere is the glacier's mark more impressive than in Wisconsin, so much so that most of the recent glacial advances and retreats of the Laurentide glacier sheet have been given the name Wisconsin.

The last glacier to flow into Wisconsin came about twenty-five thousand years ago and covered about two-thirds of the state. The glacier's leading edge divided into two bulges, one headed toward Chicago and the other, known as the Green Bay lobe, headed toward Madison some fourteen to twenty thousand years ago. The flowing ice gouged and scraped the land, leaving ridges called moraines and elongated hills called drumlins, one of which the capitol building in Madison sits on today. Everywhere the glacier went, it profoundly transformed the land.

Between 12,000 and 9,000 BCE, the glacier began its retreat to Canada, leaving huge seams of sand, gravel and clay in its wake. These deposits would form the foundations of the city that would emerge hundreds of years later. The gravel would become roads, the sand cement and the clay red and yellow brick.[1] As the glacier receded, meltwater flowed from the glacier's southwestern edge, filling the space between the edge of the ice mass and the high ground to the west of Madison with water. The result was Glacial Lake Yahara.

The glacial lake covered more than twenty-six thousand acres and was more than 100 percent larger than current lakes Mendota, Monona and Wingra combined.[2] With water levels around twelve feet above the current lake levels, Glacial Lake Yahara cut Madison's isthmus into a series of islands and peninsulas. Glacial Lake Yahara eventually broke through the glacial debris that had dammed the valley and led to its creation, causing the water levels to drop and the modern Yahara River to form, as well as lakes Mendota, Monona and Wingra. The retreat of the glacier also opened the land to settlement.

Paleo-Indians, the name given by archaeologists to the people who inhabited North America after the glacier, were likely the first humans to enter Wisconsin. They probably came to North America from Asia across the land bridge exposed by lowered sea levels in the Bering Strait twelve to fifteen thousand years ago. Paleo-Indians likely arrived in Madison about 9,500 BCE. The best evidence for these early people are the long, fluted stone projectile points they used to hunt the large ice age mammals that roamed the area, including mastodons, mammoths, bison, elk and caribou. Thousands of these points have been found in the United States, and of the hundreds discovered in Wisconsin, more have been found in Madison than in any other area of the state.

The total number of Paleo-Indians living in Wisconsin was small and spread over a large area. Developing a mobile lifestyle, they moved easily from place to place, depending on the availability of plants and animals. Although these communities spent much of their time in isolation, they did meet in larger groups at least once a year to socialize, share information, trade, hunt and conduct religious ceremonies. These meetings often occurred in spiritually charged locations, including on the lakeshores of Madison.

Between 500 BCE and 0 CE, pottery, domesticated plants, settled villages, copper tools and the practice of building earthen burial mounds were introduced to Wisconsin. These changes marked the beginning of the Woodland Tradition, named for the wooded areas of Ohio and Illinois where these changes began. In Wisconsin, the Woodland Tradition is divided into early, middle and late stages and covers the period from about 500 BCE to 1300 CE. The most dramatic Woodland influence came to Wisconsin during the late Woodland stage (about 500 CE to 1200 CE): effigy mounds.

Communities across the southern two-thirds of Wisconsin constructed these extraordinary earthen mounds, which often took the shape of animals. Some resembled birds, mammals such as bear or deer, people or spirit animals such as the thunderbird. Other mounds were abstract, including long, linear embankments or combinations of embankments with the dome-shaped mounds favored by earlier peoples. Mound sites tended to be clustered near large rivers, lakes or streams.

Judging from the number of mounds, the Madison area was a particularly attractive and special place to the Mound Builders. One scholar estimated that 98 percent of all effigy mounds found in the world are in Wisconsin, with the greatest concentration in Madison.[3] An early archaeologist counted

A four-footed Indian effigy mound on the grounds of the Mendota Mental Health Institute. *Wisconsin Historical Society Image ID #4843.*

more than 1,000 in the Madison area, with 668 around Lakes Mendota, Monona and Wingra alone. Unfortunately, most of these mounds, nearly all located on hills overlooking the water, were later vandalized, pillaged or destroyed during construction projects.

The effigy mounds puzzled early white settlers. Most were reluctant to accept that Indians could have been the creators, in part because the Indians that Europeans and Americans knew did not know much about the mounds either. There was also a bit of racism at work as many white explorers and settlers saw the Indians as savages incapable of building anything as complex as the mounds. For much of the nineteenth century, the question of who built the mounds was debated with much enthusiasm but little sound judgment. Among the people credited with building the mounds between 1820 and 1890 were the Ten Lost Tribes of Israel, forgotten European visitors, the inhabitants of Atlantis and a mythical lost race of Americans.

Many early investigations of the mounds focused on excavations, the assumption being that the mounds contained artifacts that would provide a window into the lives of their builders. Unfortunately, the mounds had few artifacts, and the excavations usually destroyed more than they uncovered. Most mounds contained human bones, and some had deposits of charcoal, ash, animal bone, shell or rock. Wisconsin's first scientist, Increase Lapham, completed the first systematic mapping and investigation of the mounds in the late 1840s, publishing his detailed recordings as *The Antiquities of Wisconsin* in 1855. Forty years later, in 1894, Cyrus Thomas published his definitive report on the mounds, proving that Indians had indeed built the mounds and laying to rest some of the more preposterous theories of the day.

Even after the question of *who* was answered, *why* the mounds were built continues to prove elusive. Some think the mounds may have served as territorial markers for the various clans that moved with seasonal changes to take advantage of nature's resources. Others propose that the earthen mounds expressed the theology and beliefs of the effigy mound culture. According to this premise, each mound group symbolized the three levels of the late Woodland universe—sky, earth and water—sculpted into the earth. Birds represented the sky spirit, the bear and other animals the earth spirit and the long-tailed creatures, sometimes turtles and panthers, the sky or underworld spirit.

It's also not clear why the Mound Builders stopped building mounds. Some archaeologists have speculated that the arrival of new Indian groups in the area led older residents to express themselves in new ways. By 900 CE, some Indian communities had also begun to settle in semipermanent villages, creating difficulty for their more mobile neighbors. Building palisades and more permanent housing required substantially more cooperative effort than remaining on the move. Others have also pointed to the expansion of corn horticulture, which may have shifted religious rituals to focus on soil fertility.

The answers to these questions may never be known. The effigy mound culture gradually transformed beyond recognition as communities adapted to the changing social and economic environment. What became of the Mound Builders is also a mystery. Many now think that the ancestors of the Ho-Chunk Indians built the mounds as so many of their oral traditions are consistent with the sky-earth-water interpretation of the mounds' meaning.

Beginning about 1650, European settlement brought even more changes to Wisconsin's Indian peoples. Eastern tribes, including the Sauk, Fox, Ottawa, Potawatomi, Kickapoo and Ojibwe, moved west to Wisconsin as white settlement increased along the East Coast of the United States. The arrival of these new tribes strained the resources available to Wisconsin's original inhabitants, causing frequent combat, territorial disputes and shifting alliances among the tribes.

When the Americans came in the early nineteenth century, the Ho-Chunk controlled the Madison area. Ho-Chunk villages were located on the shore of Lake Mendota near Fox Bluff, Tenney Park and at Picnic Point; and on Lake Monona at Frost Woods and Winnequah. The Indians fished in the lakes, harvested wild rice and cultivated corn, potatoes, pumpkins, squashes and tobacco on the isthmus. Madison's water and woodland environment was rich in everything the Indians needed to live a good life. Dozens of Indian village sites throughout the Madison area show that there was hardly a neighborhood or vista not first enjoyed by Indians. But their control over the area would soon be threatened by European settlement.

2

EUROPEAN CONTACT AND EXPLORATION

By the seventeenth century, Europeans were afoot in Wisconsin, though not necessarily in Madison. The French explored Wisconsin first. They came—and stayed—for the fur. From 1650 to 1850, Wisconsin's economy revolved around the beaver. Before the beaver, white-tailed deer, catfish and wild turkey had been the state's most valuable animals, supporting human communities for more than ten thousand years. After 1650, the beaver reigned supreme.

The reason was simple: hats. From Russia to London to the French Riviera, Europe's most fashionable people preferred hats made from beaver. The waterproof fur could be shaved and pressed into felt that kept the wearer both warm and dry. Demand for beaver hats remained immense for more than two hundred years, so anyone who could supply beaver pelts could grow rich. French demand for beaver was nearly matched by Indian desire for European products, including knives, awls, kettles, cloth, ammunition and alcohol. The French fur trade came to quickly dominate Indian life, especially as many Indian groups began to rely on imported technology to carry out their daily tasks. Soon, most of the basic necessities of Indian life could only be provided by the French, and for those goods, the traders demanded furs.

Fur was not the only motivating factor for French exploration. The desire to save souls also brought the French to Wisconsin. Missionaries arrived soon after the traders, and though their motives were quite different, they often found themselves working closely together. While the traders received furs from the Indians, the Jesuit priests set up missions to convert the Indians to Christianity. Conflict between spirituality and commerce was inevitable, however, and by the early 1700s, the Jesuits were expelled, and the French soldiers, who guarded the lucrative trade routes, held power in Wisconsin until late in the century.

Whether the French fur traders made it to Madison during their reign is not known. But their influence on the growth of the state is undeniable. The interior fur trade was so profitable that the English tried for years to win Indian suppliers away from the French, resulting in the French and Indian War. Between 1755 and 1763, the French and English fought pitched battles from Quebec to Pennsylvania. In the end, the French lost, and with the signing of the Treaty of Paris, a large area that included Wisconsin became British territory.

The British lost Wisconsin a few decades later in the Revolutionary War, although the Americans did not begin to assert their control until after the War of 1812. The new American government had many more important priorities than the remote Wisconsin frontier in its early years, so French and British traders continued to operate unfettered in Wisconsin. That changed with the War of 1812.

Realizing that Wisconsin and its fur trade needed protection, the Americans built a series of military outposts that stretched from Canada to the Gulf Coast. Three were in Wisconsin: Fort Howard at Green Bay (1816), Fort Winnebago at Portage (1828) and Fort Crawford at Prairie du Chien (1816). One year after Fort Crawford was built, John Jacob Astor brought his American Fur Company to Wisconsin, employing Pierre Paquette as his agent for the Madison area. The heyday of the fur trade was coming to an end, however.

The last fur-collecting effort made around Madison occurred between 1829 and 1835. American Wallace Rowan set up his trading operation on the north shore of Lake Mendota near Pheasant Branch Creek about 1830. His log cabin became the earliest-known permanent home in the Madison area, and his wife, the first known white woman to enter the area. He later moved to Winnequah on the eastern shore of Lake Monona. Another American trader, Abel Rasdall, set up his trading post on the shores of Lake Kegonsa in 1831. Rasdall had another trading post on what is today Pinckney Street on the Capitol Square.

Two French traders were also working in Madison at the same time. Michael St. Cyr took over Rowan's cabin with his Ho-Chunk wife in 1833. The other Frenchman, Oliver Armel, set up his trading operation near the intersection of Johnson Street and Wisconsin Avenue. The French did not stay long in Madison, however. The line of American settlement was moving rapidly westward, threatening the traders' livelihoods. By 1838, nearly all the traders had moved west.

Beginning in the late 1820s, other Americans were finding reasons aside from fur to come to Madison. Ebenezer Brigham came west in 1818, migrating to Platteville in 1827. Sometime in the spring of 1828, Brigham spent a night in Madison on his way to Fort Winnebago, camping on the Capitol Square. He was so struck by what he called the "strange beauty of the place" that he predicted a village or city would grow up there.[4] That same year, Brigham settled near Moundville (today's Blue Mounds), becoming the first permanent settler in Dane County.

A visitor far more significant to Madison's future passed through the area in 1829. James Duane Doty, a territorial judge in Michigan with jurisdiction from Mackinac to the Mississippi, passed through Madison on his way between Green Bay and Prairie du Chien. Doty traveled with Green Bay attorneys Henry S. Baird and Morgan L. Martin, two men who would figure prominently in early Wisconsin politics. Doty normally made the trip by canoe along the Fox and Wisconsin Rivers but decided to travel overland this time to expand his knowledge of the state. That trip eventually led to his purchase of much of what became downtown Madison.

By 1830, Madison was no longer unknown to white explorers and settlers, though few white settlers or explorers actually visited. The most notable people to pass through Madison next were Indians in a desperate attempt at escape during the Black Hawk War in 1832.

The war that erupted in Wisconsin in 1832 traced its origins to events in St. Louis in 1804. At the time, future president William Henry Harrison negotiated a treaty with two representatives of the Sauk Nation who had come to the city on other business. When it was over, the government believed it had secured the right to open all Sauk lands east of the Mississippi to settlement, some fifty million acres of land in what is now northern Illinois and southern Wisconsin. The treaty allowed the Sauk to remain on the land until the government actually sold the land to settlers, however.

A quarter of a century later, with lead being profitably mined from the Rock River region, thousands of settlers swarmed into the area. Keokuk, a widely respected Sauk leader, thought it was futile to resist the tide of settlement and agreed to move across the Mississippi River to Iowa in return for enough corn to get through the winter. But when the government failed to honor its promises concerning the move, a group of about twelve hundred Sauk under the leadership of Black Hawk (*Ma-ka-tai-me-she-kia-kiak*) returned to the Illinois side of the river in hopes of reoccupying their homeland and harvesting their corn.

Black Hawk believed the 1804 treaty fraudulent, arguing that the two negotiators had never possessed the authority to speak for the whole Sauk Nation. Once back across the river, Black Hawk hoped to form an alliance with the Ho-Chunk, Kickapoo, Potawatomi and other disaffected Indian groups in Wisconsin and Illinois. He also thought the British might come to his aid in the event of a full-scale war with the Americans. None of his hopes came true, however. The Americans, unsurprisingly, saw Black Hawk's return as a hostile invasion and sent the Illinois militia and the U.S. Army to greet him and his followers in the summer of 1832.

Returning to the Sauk village of Saukenuk in northwestern Illinois, Black Hawk found his people's cornfields trampled by cattle and the land fenced in by settlers. The American forces tried to pin down the Sauk, but beginning with the Battle of Stillman's Run on May 14, 1832, the Indians managed to evade capture repeatedly as they attempted to retreat to Iowa.

For sixteen weeks, Black Hawk and his warriors created tactical diversions while the Sauk women and children tried to make their way safely back across the Mississippi. They led the Americans on a circuitous route from Illinois into Wisconsin, a route that passed right through the future site of downtown Madison.

Reaching Madison on July 20, the Americans decided to camp for the night near Olbrich Park. Their guide, Pierre Paquette, had warned them that the isthmus was covered in dense underbrush, a situation that greatly favored the Sauk. Knowing that the Americans were close behind them, the Sauk had split in two, with a group of warriors camped near the west side of the Yahara River to attack the Americans if they tried to cross the river during the night. The main group of Sauk had camped on the east shore of Lake Mendota near Pheasant Branch Creek.[5]

General Henry Atkinson was given the charge of chasing down the Sauk for the Americans. Atkinson had fought in the War of 1812 and led expeditions to the far West before being put in charge of the three thousand U.S. forces pursuing Black Hawk. The Sauk proved a frustratingly elusive target for Atkinson, as his men went weeks without finding Black Hawk before discovering the fresh trail that proved he was headed toward the Mississippi by way of Madison.

Several attempts to surrender by the Sauk were rebuffed or misinterpreted by the American troops during their flight. Supplies of food and water repeatedly ran out as Black Hawk attempted to hide in the marshy lowlands. Many very young or elderly Indians died of hunger, thirst and exhaustion and were buried on the trail. In the worst instances, an occasional straggler was left behind to await death. Warriors skirmished with the Wisconsin militia often enough to keep them at bay, but these fights also kindled fear amongst settlers and a desire for revenge in the minds of the soldiers.

Finally, on August 1, 1832, twelve days after Black Hawk had passed through Madison, the surviving Sauk reached the banks of the Mississippi River near the mouth of the Bad Axe River. Attempting to cross to safety, the Sauk were caught in the crossfire between a gunboat on the river ahead of them and the pursuing troops on the bluffs behind them. Black Hawk again attempted a white flag of truce but was rebuffed by the Americans. More than 900 of Black Hawk's people were killed in the Battle of Bad Axe, the Mississippi River running red with blood. About 70 Sauk made it across the river, only to be killed by Sioux warriors, longtime enemies of the Sauk who were fighting on the side of the Americans. At least 250 American soldiers and settlers died as well.[6]

Small groups of Sauk hid after the battle in the woods or in the hunting camps of sympathetic Ho-Chunk. Of Black Hawk's initial community of 1,200 followers, only about 150 Sauk survived. Black Hawk surrendered to authorities at Fort Crawford after facing the rebuke of his council.

The Black Hawk War left an impression on Americans and Indians. The display of overwhelming power by the U.S. troops convinced most other Wisconsin Indian nations that Keokuk had been right and that military resistance to the U.S. government was hopeless. For Americans, the war further solidified their hatred and distrust of Indians.

One month after the Black Hawk War, the Americans summoned Ho-Chunk chiefs to Fort Armstrong at Rock Island, Illinois. There, the government demanded the cession of all Ho-Chunk lands between the Wisconsin River and the Rock River, an area that included Madison. No Ho-

Chunk could legally reside there after June 1, 1833, according to the terms of the Rock Island Treaty.[7] They weren't the only ones losing their land. Soon, the Sauk, Fox, Potawatomi and Ottawa also gave up their lands east of the Mississippi and left the state. By 1840, most of Wisconsin belonged to the Americans rather than its original inhabitants.

The Ho-Chunk in the Madison area faced dim prospects. The Black Hawk War had prevented them from planting their usual crops, and game was scarce, so they had no food for the winter. Many starved to death.

In the spring of 1833, the Ho-Chunk asked the Indian agents if they could stay in Madison and harvest one last crop, promising to then leave without trouble. The memories of war and fear of Indians were too great to allow them to stay, however. Colonel Henry Dodge called a meeting with the Ho-Chunk chiefs on the north shore of Lake Mendota to negotiate the details of their removal in April. Dodge rejected their plea to remain in the Madison area but did agree to have several loads of corn delivered to them. He also arranged for wagons to transport their belongings to the Wisconsin River.[8]

On the evening before their removal, the Ho-Chunk held a medicine dance ceremony near Madison. The Indian agent gave them some presents, and their belongings were loaded onto the wagons for transport to Sauk Prairie. Many members were reluctant to leave, and it took almost to the end of 1833 for the Americans to finally clear the holdouts.

And just in time, for American settlement could not be held back from Wisconsin for much longer. Land surveyors began dividing up Wisconsin into blocks of land in 1832, beginning at a point on the Wisconsin-Illinois border about ten miles east of the Mississippi. Southern Wisconsin was surveyed between 1833 and 1835. Town 7, Range 9 East, the land out of which Madison would be carved, was completed in December 1834.[9] Speculators pounced on surveyor notes and maps looking for desirable tracts to purchase for resale.

The first road across southern Wisconsin, connecting Fort Crawford in Prairie du Chien with Fort Winnebago at Portage, was completed in 1835. The road passed close to Madison, nearly touching the north shore of Lake Mendota.

The road was the work of James Duane Doty, the Michigan judge who had visited Madison in 1829. Doty had argued that Fort Winnebago could be neither protected nor supplied without a road connecting it to Fort

Crawford and Fort Howard in Green Bay. He also argued that such a road was essential to territorial settlement, a major preoccupation of Americans in Wisconsin. Doty not only convinced the United States Congress to appropriate the funds, but he also got himself appointed as one of two commissioners charged with laying out the road.

By 1836, when Wisconsin became a territory, the foundations were nearly laid for American settlement. The Indians were mostly gone (and those who remained were largely subdued), the land had been surveyed and a road linking Madison to the biggest population centers of the new territory had been constructed.

3

CAPITAL CITY

On August 1, 1835, land in and around Madison went on sale at the federal land office in Green Bay. An acre of land could be had for just $1.25. Buyers could buy as many parcels of land as they wanted, but no less than a quarter section. Strangely, the first land parcels to sell were not the waterfront lots on the isthmus that are so appealing today; in fact, no one purchased land on the isthmus until October.

Most of the eventual purchasers were not hardworking farmers or settlers looking to make a new start. Instead, they were wealthy investors who hoped to strike it rich on land speculation. Historian David Mollenhoff reports that astute land purchases could rise in value between 100 and 700 percent in just twelve to eighteen months, profit potential enough to whet the appetite of many an investor.

After five months of land office sales, only two pieces of land on the isthmus had sold. Eastern investor Frances Tillou had purchased one hundred acres to the east of the isthmus where the Yahara River empties into Lake Monona. The other purchaser was James Duane Doty, the former territorial judge and active Wisconsin promoter in the Michigan legislature. He bought a parcel on both sides of the Yahara River between Tenney Park and East Washington Avenue.

Even unsold, the available land between the lakes did not go unnoticed. In January 1836, twelve Wisconsin members of the Michigan legislature, including Doty, held a meeting in Green Bay to discuss separating Wisconsin from the

James Duane Doty convinced the territorial legislature to select Madison as Wisconsin's capital. *Wisconsin Historical Society Image ID #11337.*

Michigan territory. Doty discussed the potential advantages of locating a town on the isthmus. The group agreed to inspect the site for future purchase.

A few months later, Doty traveled to Detroit to visit his old friend and newly elected Michigan territorial governor Steven T. Mason. Doty and Mason discussed good land investments in Wisconsin, and the subject of the isthmus naturally arose. They agreed to purchase about one thousand acres of the isthmus, centered on the point where the capitol now stands, for about $1,500. Doty organized a joint stock company known as the Four Lakes Company, which combined his land with those acres owned by Frances Tillou, the other early isthmus land investor, to divide and sell the property. Doty now had near absolute control over the isthmus and its future.

On July 4, 1836, the Wisconsin Territory was born. Doty had hoped to be appointed governor of the new territory, but President Andrew Jackson chose his rival, Henry Dodge, instead. Dodge was a respected leader from the lead mining region who had distinguished himself during the Black Hawk War as colonel of the Iowa County militia.[10] The new governor had the responsibility of conducting a census, holding elections and convening a territorial legislature.

Dodge acted quickly in his new role. The census was taken in August and found 11,683 non-Indian residents between Lake Michigan and the Dakotas. Elections in early October chose delegates for a territorial convention. The winners of that election first met in a chilly, wood-framed building at Belmont in southwestern Wisconsin on October 25, 1836. The most important item on their agenda was the selection of a capital.[11]

Competition for the capital site had grown fierce since the meeting in Green Bay in January. Land speculators knew that winning this coveted prize was a sure path to riches, so town promoters came to Belmont bearing maps of prospective cities, each more beautiful and attractive than the next.

Out of political office, Doty, too, had begun work on his own plan for a capital city. On his way to Belmont, Doty brought along Green Bay surveyor John V. Suydam to measure and sketch out a hypothetical city on the isthmus. If the territorial delegation chose Madison for the capital, Doty and his partners stood to earn a windfall.

Describing their stay on the isthmus, Suydam later wrote:

> *While standing at the section corner, on that beautiful spot between the Lakes, then the central point of a wilderness...I have no doubt Gov. Doty*

> *saw in his far-reaching mind...a splendid city surrounding the capitol of Wisconsin at Four Lakes.*

Immediately after arriving in Belmont, Doty began giving Suydam "minute directions as to its whole plan," every part of which was designed to take advantage of the area's topography.[12] The plan that resulted was not, as historian David Mollenhoff writes, "a model of surveying precision." Some of the blocks were only half as deep as the survey indicated, while others were, in fact, completely under water. The plan also called for a canal at the narrowest point of the isthmus, a proposal that would have required a gorge through a hill forty feet high at some points.[13] As the finishing touches were put on the plan for "Madison City," Doty began to lobby on its behalf.

The question of where to place the capital ignited fierce debate in the legislature. Some argued for putting it near a center of population, such as in the lead region near Mineral Point or at Green Bay. Promoters of smaller areas, such as Milwaukee, which at the time consisted of little more than a single log cabin, lobbied on the basis of future prospects. Others thought the capital should be in a central location. Since half the population of the new territory lived in Iowa and Minnesota, that meant a capital on the Mississippi River. Doty used every means at his disposal to convince delegates to select Madison. And as the only person who had actually visited most of the proposed sites—among them Mineral Point, Milwaukee, Fond du Lac, Portage, Racine, Platteville and Koshkonong—his word carried some weight.

Doty was also adept at other means of persuasion. "There probably never was a legislature met at any place with poorer accommodations than this legislature had at Belmont," Iowa politician Hawkins Taylor recalled. Many members slept on frigid bare floors in the hastily constructed village. Doty arrived armed with a full stock of buffalo robes, which he passed around to the members, making them as comfortable as possible until he had secured enough votes. He also freely distributed Madison town lots to legislators and their friends.[14]

The name of his proposed town, Madison, was also appealing. The revered president and founding father James Madison had died just five months before the Belmont session. Doty capitalized on sentimental feelings of the time by selecting Madison as the name for his town. Adding to the town's patriotic plumage, Doty named all the streets after signers of the U.S. Constitution and gave the name Washington to the city's main thoroughfare.[15]

When the question of the capital came up for discussion on November 21 in the council (the equivalent of today's senate), the debate raged for two days. On the twenty-third, a draft bill naming Madison the capital was introduced for a vote, but a spirited attack led to motions to strike out Madison in favor of fifteen other places. All were voted down. Finally, late in the afternoon, the council chose Madison by a vote of seven to six.

In the House of Representatives, the opposition was less formidable, though the debate went on for hours. Representatives finally approved Madison by a vote of fifteen to eleven. Nineteen sites had been nominated, but only Madison remained.

Doty's shrewd maneuvers didn't end there. Two months after Madison was selected as the territorial capital, Doty created Madison's first suburb, a nine-hundred-acre subdivision known as the Western Addition. Prominent in its design was "Seminary Square," a space set aside for a university along Lake Mendota. An 1838 bill introduced in the legislature called for a territorial university to be located in or near Madison. The suburb failed to materialize, defeated by an economic depression, but the plan did impress in people's minds that a university should be located on Madison's western edge. People even began referring to the area just east of Seminary Square as "College Hill," and in 1848, the first regents purchased the area for the campus of the state university.

In the months that followed, the capitol grounds were established on Madison's highest hill. Major streets were laid out, buildings were erected and speculators from as far away as New York and Washington, D.C., bought lots. From their initial $1,500 investment, Doty and his partners ultimately made $35,510, a handsome return on an eight-month investment.

4
FRONTIER LIFE

Even after Madison became the new territorial capital, there was, with apologies to Gertrude Stein, no there there. Fewer than forty white settlers lived in all of Dane County, and none lived in Madison in late 1836. The first white family to move to Madison arrived on a snowy Saturday in April 1837.

Eben and Rosaline Peck learned of Madison's selection as the territorial capital in December 1836, when several Green Bay men who had attended the session at Belmont stopped in their Blue Mounds tavern. Hearing the news, the Pecks saw an opportunity. Construction crews hired to build the new capitol, as well as visitors, would need a place to stay and eat. The Pecks decided to close their Blue Mounds tavern to open a public house in Madison. They purchased two lots for $100 each from men who had purchased the same lots only nineteen days before for $5 each.[16] Eben arranged to have two cabins built on the property.

A few months later, Eben, a pregnant Rosaline and their son, Victor, left Blue Mounds for Madison. They arrived on April 15, 1837. Eben quickly set to work constructing a structure to connect the two cabins and a kitchen, anticipating the large crew of construction workers on their way to build the city from the ground up.[17]

Their first customers arrived in May. Fifteen men from Milwaukee charged with blazing a trail for the capitol workmen who would soon follow enjoyed the Pecks' hospitality for several days. One month later, on June

10, 1837, the capitol construction crew under the direction of Augustus A. Bird arrived in Madison. A few hours later, Simeon Mills, a man destined to become Madison's first great entrepreneur, arrived at Lake Monona, having followed Indian trails and surveyor marks from Chicago.

Construction projects blossomed with the arrival of new people. A dormitory to house the workers was constructed on the capitol square near the King Street corner, and a boardinghouse came up at the corner of Butler and Wilson Streets. Some of the workmen opted to build their own cabins rather than pay rent. Simeon Mills built Madison's first store at the corner of Webster and Main. On the Fourth of July 1837, Madison residents celebrated the nation's sixty-first independence day by laying the cornerstone of the territorial capitol.

A few months later, on September 14, Rosaline Peck gave birth to a daughter, the first non-Indian child born in Madison. Doty suggested that they name the child Wisconsina in honor of the new territory. Simeon Mills suggested Victoria in honor of the young queen who had recently ascended the English throne. The Pecks took both suggestions and named their daughter Victoria Wisconsina.[18]

The rest of 1837 passed uneventfully. Most everyone spent their time working, chopping, sawing and digging a town out of the wilderness. When construction on the capitol stopped for the winter, Madison's population plummeted. Most of the workmen returned to Milwaukee, leaving only four families, a few stray workmen, a couple shopkeepers and a handful of officials.

A year later, when legislators met in Madison for the first legislative session held in the new capitol, about thirty buildings stood on the stump-strewn hillside centered on King Street. Of the people living in Madison, the city's first white residents, the Pecks, were no longer among them.

One year of work as innkeepers had left Eben and Rosaline exhausted. They sold their tavern to Robert L. Ream in 1838 and moved to an eighty-acre farm one mile from Madison. Ream renamed the tavern the Madison House and offered two rooms to rent for the incoming legislators. The Madison Hotel and the brand-new American Hotel also had rooms to let.

Besides rooms, the American Hotel also served as makeshift legislative chambers, as the capitol building remained far from finished. After weeks of meeting in the hotel's basement, a committee declared the capitol's legislative chambers ready for use. Based on one participant's recollections, the determination may have been a bit premature:

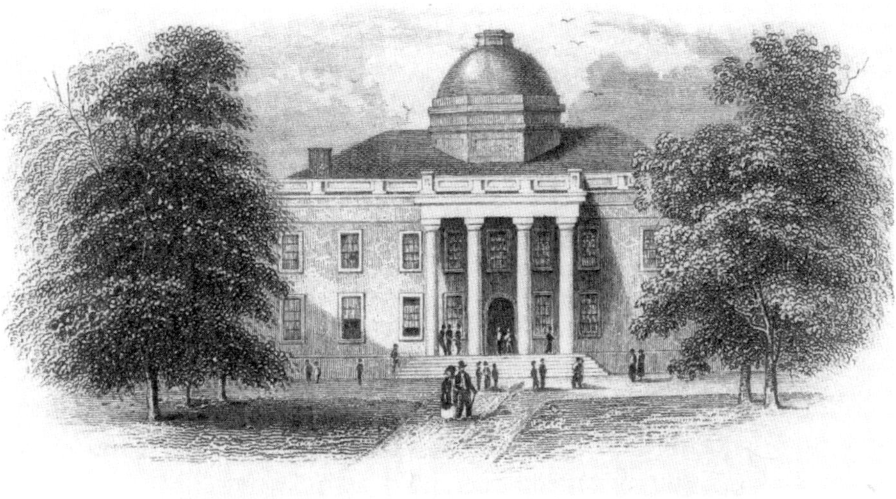

Madison's first capitol building was more than just a center of state government; it also served as a dance hall, theater, church, meeting hall and funeral parlor. *Wisconsin Historical Society Image ID 7042.*

> *The floors were laid with green oak boards full of ice; the walls of the room were iced over; green oak seats and desks made of rough boards; one fire-place and one small stove. In a few days the flooring near the stove and fire-place so shrunk on account of the heat that a person could run his hands between the boards. The basement story was all open, and James Morrison's large droves of hogs had taken possession. The weather was cold, the halls were cold, our ink would freeze—so that when we could stand it no longer we passed a joint resolution to adjourn for twenty days.*[19]

When the legislature reconvened, the capitol was more habitable, though the pigs remained. The pigs' owner, James Morrison, had come to Madison to build the capitol and never left. He opened a store and built the American House hotel. Since he'd built the capitol, perhaps he felt he had the right to keep his pigs beneath it.

The pigs remained for at least a decade and sometimes proved quite useful. One day, a legislator, deciding that the session had gone on long enough, made a motion to adjourn. When his motion was voted down, the legislator seized a long pole and poked it down between the cracks in the rough floorboards. There "ensued a chorus of grunts and squeals and the sound of trampling feet made by the pigs…Such clouds of dust began to rise between the cracks in the floor that the lawmakers began sneezing and coughing. The session was soon adjourned."[20]

The capitol was finally finished in 1844. It received mostly flattering remarks, praised for its "splendid yellow stone" and shiny tin-covered dome. What wasn't praised was its cost—nearly twice as much as had been budgeted.[21]

The capitol's budget overrun created a major scandal and certainly didn't help quell calls to move the capital to a new spot, usually Milwaukee. Annoyed with the primitive conditions in both the city and in their chambers, legislators introduced bills to take the capital away from Madison nearly every year. These efforts were rebuffed, but not without considerable effort on the part of Madison residents. Supporters of moving the capital to Milwaukee regularly opposed all improvements to the Madison capitol because these investments only increased resistance to their cause.[22]

The relocation efforts weren't the only difficulties facing the frontier city. John Mason Peck's popular emigrant guide to western settlement, *A New Guide for Emigrants to the West* (1836), employed Edenic visual descriptors of the West but did warn that settlers "should take it for granted that there are difficulties to be encountered." For those willing to take a chance on Madison, this meant distance, poor roads, high prices, sickness, Indians, prairie fires and mosquitoes.

Surrounded by lakes and marshes, lacking good transportation routes and far from major cities, Madison did not offer easy access to markets for farmers. Settlement in southern Wisconsin happened first along Lake Michigan and in the lead mining area, leaving huge strips of farmland between these areas and Madison that had to be filled. Farmers had little incentive to grow crops in Madison if they then had to haul them more than eighty miles to Milwaukee over poor roads.

Land was also expensive. Speculation had driven land prices beyond what many settlers could afford. Even those who could buy land faced high prices for food and other goods because nearly everything had to be shipped in from Milwaukee or Mineral Point.

Residents suffered from their share of frontier sicknesses. Malaria swept through in 1844–45, and there were several cases of typhoid fever. Horace Tenney, who arrived in Madison in 1845, claimed that he caught malaria, which left him feverish, lethargic and chilled for a decade.[23] Woe to those who became sick in the early years, though, as the closest doctor was nearly forty miles away at Fort Winnebago.

The Ho-Chunk Indians continued to live near Madison, despite being officially banished by the U.S. government. Most settlers regarded them with suspicion and disgust, believing that the Indians had no right to be there.

Wind-driven prairie fires caused some of the greatest terror among settlers. Newspaper accounts and reminiscences describe fires that roared across the isthmus. One early settler told the *Wisconsin State Journal* on February 4, 1870, that "prairie fires coming down over the distant hills, on all sides toward the lakes afforded a spectacle for which one could dispense with all the circuses and fat women shows that will ever be sent wandering among us." At night, the flames were sometimes visible twenty miles away on the horizon.[24]

Mosquitoes, often jokingly called Wisconsin's state bird, were no less vicious in the nineteenth century. Simeon Mills proclaimed that "there probably never was a place on this broad earth worse infested" with mosquitoes than Madison.[25] Settlers and visitors reported swarms of mosquitoes so thick that they could barely hunt, take a swim or sleep without the incessant whine.

Despite all these difficulties, Madison still managed to attract 238 people in its first ten years. This growth was strikingly slow, however, compared to other places in Wisconsin. Milwaukee, for example, had a population of 1,712 in 1840; ten years later, in 1850, the population was 20,061. Madison, by contrast, grew from 146 people in 1840 to fewer than 300 by 1845.

Madison's slow growth frustrated its residents. King Street continued to be the center of town, though King Street itself, the only clearly defined street, was still filled with stumps in 1846, just as it had been in 1838. Hunters regularly tracked birds and other game in the dense forests of Mansion Hill. A large marsh on the east end of the isthmus became so waterlogged in the spring that fishermen could spear huge catches in the shallow waters. Even in their irritation, the settlers did express appreciation for the beauty of the wilderness around them. "Language cannot paint the intoxicating beauty of this garden of the world before it was touched by the utilizing hand of civilization," recalled Simeon Mills.

Most early Madison residents were young and came from New England and New York. Storekeeper and entrepreneur Simeon Mills came to Madison from Connecticut when he was twenty-seven years old. Vermonters Eben and Rosaline Peck came to Madison when they were twenty-nine and thirty-three years old, respectively. Madison's first postmaster, John Catlin, also from Vermont, was thirty-five. James Duane Doty came west from New York and convinced the legislature to pick Madison as the capital when he was thirty-seven years old.

Despite their isolation, settlers still found much about their frontier life idyllic and happy. Unlike many other frontier communities, Madison had enough women to support community dances. The Madison Lyceum, begun by Darwin Clark, a member of the capitol construction crew, held debates on a variety of topics and fed the deep-seated Yankee desire for mental improvement.

The only real crime that occurred in Madison's first decade happened in the territorial legislature. In 1842, Grant County representative James R. Vineyard shot Brown County legislator Charles P. Arndt dead on the council floor. Vineyard was immediately expelled from the legislature but was somehow found not guilty of murder. Charles Dickens, who was touring the United States at the time, cited the incident in his *American Notes for General Circulation* (1842) as an example of the rampant lawlessness on the U.S. frontier.[26]

Madison grew slowly during its early years, but as it did, the three part-time county commissioners found themselves hard pressed to provide the capital city with much attention or money. Within a few years, Madison had grown large enough to need its own laws and its own money for schools, roads, fire equipment and other services.

In December 1845, citizens met to endorse the idea of incorporating Madison as a village. Two months later, in February 1846, the territorial legislature approved the village charter. For the first time, Madison could make its own laws and create its own tax base.

5

BECOMING A CITY

Little more than a wilderness outpost with a handful of residents in 1846, Madison became a thriving, prosperous town only ten years later. Leading the charge was a successful Milwaukee hardware merchant who bought large pieces of land on the east isthmus from James Duane Doty in 1847. At the time of his purchase, nearly everyone could make a good case for Madison's potential as a city, but it needed a champion, someone willing to take a risk and gamble on Madison's future. That someone was the indefatigable Leonard J. Farwell.[27]

Farwell came to Madison at a precipitous moment. Farmers were finally converging on Madison, having moved west from Milwaukee and east from the Mississippi River. Land prices finally fell to a point more affordable to settlers and farmers after a decade of slow land sales due to speculation. In 1848, one year after Farwell's purchase, Wisconsin became a state, and Madison was made the state's permanent capital, ending, at least for the time being, the campaign to move the capital. Madison also became home to the University of Wisconsin and, in 1852, the State Insane Asylum, major boons to a fledgling village. All of these developments suggested that Madison's hour might have finally arrived.

Farwell came to Madison in 1848, eager for the challenge of making a second fortune in a new town. He had come west from New York at the age of nineteen, settling in Lockport, Illinois, where he ran a successful hardware store. In 1840, he moved to Milwaukee, where he started his own firm, L.J. Farwell and Company, which, within a few years, had become one of the largest hardware companies in the west.[28] In 1848, after embarking on an extensive foreign tour of Africa, Asia and Europe, Farwell returned to Wisconsin, sold his Milwaukee business and moved to Madison. He was soon leading his new hometown toward spectacular growth.

Over the next eight years, Farwell straightened the Yahara River and harnessed the water power of Lake Mendota to run Madison Mills, a flour mill with an attached sawmill completed in 1851.[29] He opened Williamson Street and Fort Winnebago Road (today's Milwaukee Street) and drained parts of the huge marsh between the capitol and the Yahara River for more streets. He also served as an officer of the Dane County Bank and of the Madison Gas, Light and Coke Company.

Farwell didn't just develop Madison—he also extensively promoted it. He worked closely with immigration agents in the eastern United States to encourage German immigrants to settle in Madison. He created pamphlets and maps, which he distributed in the East and in Europe, that emphasized Madison's business opportunities and natural beauty.[30]

Farwell even convinced the legislature to change the names of the lakes. Government surveyors had labeled the lakes with numbers in the 1830s. While preparing a promotional map of the city, Farwell sought to give the lakes more romantic names, names more reminiscent of the Indians who had long lived in the area. Ethnologist and surveyor Frank Hudson suggested the names Mendota and Monona. Lyman Draper, secretary of the State Historical Society of Wisconsin, suggested Waubesa and Kegonsa for the other two lakes. Although meant to sound Indian, none was a name that the Indians ever gave to the lakes (the Ho-Chunk referred to the lakes as *Tay-cho-per-ah*, or the "Four Lakes").[31] The new names were officially approved by the legislature in February 1855.

Even as he was helping to build Madison, Farwell was also helping to build his own career by becoming active in local politics. In 1852, he became Wisconsin's youngest governor at the age of thirty-three. During his two-year term, Farwell established the state geological survey, abolished the death penalty, created the Institute for the Education of the Deaf and Dumb in Delavan and reorganized the State Historical Society of Wisconsin. Work crews filled and graded East Washington Avenue from Blount Street to the Yahara River and built Madison's first plank-paved road. Farwell also created the State Commission of Immigration to actively encourage European emigration to Wisconsin. The commission was so successful in expanding European settlement that the model was adopted by several other states.[32]

To run Madison while he also ran the state, Farwell hired Harlow S. Orton to handle daily gubernatorial business. Orton was later elected mayor of Madison and served on the Wisconsin Supreme Court. Giving Orton control of the day-to-day activities gave Farwell the time to devote to keeping Madison growing.

Farwell also built himself a magnificent mansion on the south end of Brearly Street near Lake Monona. The three-story octagonal stone house was nearly nine thousand square feet in size and was the fanciest house in town when it was finished in 1854. A small enclave of Yankee businessmen soon built their homes in the area, though none could rival the scale and expense of Farwell's home.[33]

Describing Farwell in his *History of Madison*, Daniel Durrie wrote:

> *Perhaps no one person did more to promote the interests of Madison than* [Farwell]…*No important interest, structure, or association was inaugurated which he either did not originate or contribute to its success by his means or influence.*

While Farwell's accomplishments greatly encouraged settlement and improved public infrastructure, perhaps his biggest success was inspiring confidence in Madison's future prospects. That future was also greatly helped by the arrival of the railroad in 1854.

Railroads could make or break a town in the mid-nineteenth century, so towns competed vigorously for the attention of railroad companies. Canals, once the great hope for the Wisconsin frontier, had proven far too costly and difficult to construct. Roads were undependable and often impassable in bad weather. Trains, on the other hand, traveled at faster speeds and in all kinds of weather and, by the 1840s, seemed the only option to improve transportation to many in Wisconsin.

Railroads had proven themselves in the eastern United States, and by the early 1840s, there was already talk of constructing a continental railroad uniting the Atlantic and the Pacific. The opening of the Chicago–Galena line stirred the Wisconsin legislature into action. In 1847, the legislature authorized a train line from Milwaukee to Waukesha that was later extended to the Mississippi River.

As the capital city, Madison did not have to gamble on its future to get its first railroad as other towns did. Residents purchased railroad stock beginning in the late 1840s to fund the railroads. Finally, on May 23, 1854, the first train steamed into the Madison depot, greeted by more than two thousand people.[34]

The benefits of the train were immediately evident. Within days of the line's opening, twenty-five- to thirty-car trains filled with Madison wheat traveled to Milwaukee. Travel through town doubled in the summer of 1854, and an entire village of support structures—warehouses, taverns and other businesses—grew up around the depot.[35]

Amidst all this development, Madison's population boomed: from about six hundred people in 1846 to nine thousand in 1856. The surge in population led to the growth of several new areas of settlement: Mansion Hill, Tenney-Lapham (then known as Fourth Lake Ridge), Marquette (then Third Lake Ridge), Bassett and State Street.[36] Strangely, lakefront property remained nearly vacant. The Lake Mendota lakeshore from Tenney Park to the University of Wisconsin was largely empty in 1855, as the wealthy favored corner lots on the interior of the isthmus for their fancy homes.

Business flourished. The *Wisconsin State Journal* reported that twenty-five new stores opened in 1856 alone. Large fancy business blocks formed, and a steamship began offering fishing excursions and pleasure rides on Lake Mendota. Bumper crops and inflated prices made boom times for farmers, too.

As Madison grew, the limitations of the 1846 village charter became increasingly problematic. The property tax limit of $5 per $1,000 of assessed value made it difficult for the village to adequately address streets and sidewalks, schools, sanitation and fire protection. Jurisdictional disputes stemming from the village charter led to conflicts over poll and road taxes and the licensing and taxing of taverns. Representation on the county board was also unfairly apportioned, with Madison receiving the same number of representatives as a town with fewer than one hundred people.

The only way to solve these problems was to become a city. But despite all the arguments in its favor, the first effort to incorporate in 1852 failed. It wasn't until 1856 that Farwell, now a village trustee, stepped in to push Madison forward once again. He persuaded the village board to draft a new charter and to submit it to the legislature for approval. The legislature approved the charter on March 7, 1856.

One month later, the new mayor and twelve aldermen met in the new county courthouse, built in 1849, to organize a new city government.

6

CIVIL WAR MADISON

On April 7, 1856, businessman Jairus C. Fairchild was sworn in as Madison's first mayor. In his inaugural address to the common council, Fairchild declared, "We commence our city under most favorable circumstances…We can fix no limit to our growth and we challenge the world to produce a location for a city whose position embraces so many practical advantages."[37] Despite such optimistic projections—a sentiment only echoed in newspapers and by succeeding mayor A.A. Bird—the new city soon found itself in dire financial straits on the eve of a national crisis.

Just days after the Madison city charter went into effect, the common council approved a $100,000 bond issue to fund the immediate accoutrements of a new city: a city hall, fire protection services, schoolhouses, a cemetery and a hospital.[38] For some residents, this was an extraordinary amount of money to spend in a single year, especially considering that only a year before, leaders had refused to borrow $10,000 to build new schools. But the common council, swayed by what many believed to be Madison's prosperous future, went ahead with the bond measure.

High expectations and Madison's continuing boom led the council to approve another $100,000 in January 1857. This time, the goal was to secure a second railroad to compete with the Milwaukee and Mississippi Railroad. That railroad had come to Madison to wide acclaim in 1854 but had since left users increasingly dissatisfied with its high fares.[39] So when the Watertown and Madison Railroad formally requested $100,000 in December 1856, the council leapt into action; it also certainly did not hurt that Mayor Fairchild had just been elected president of the Watertown and Madison Railroad Company. The council approved a referendum on the issue, and the voters approved the bond soon after.

Two months later, the city dropped another $50,000, this time in a desperate measure to keep the capital in Madison. Governor Coles Bashford had issued the threat this time, stating that the capitol either be improved or moved to a new site. The council quickly approved a bond measure to fireproof and enlarge the building.[40]

With the initial $100,000 loan plus the $100,000 railroad and $50,000 capital loans, plus a $10,000 bond for a city cemetery, Madison soon found itself facing a staggering $260,000 debt. Few people seemed to care all that much, however, as economic times remained good in the new city. But things were about to change as the investment bubble in western lands burst on eastern speculators, making debts incurred in more prosperous times difficult to repay.

The first signs of a financial problem in Madison began to appear in late 1856. Sales of the $100,000 city bond had only managed to bring in $79,000, and the chair of the finance committee leading the bond drive, Napoleon Bonaparte Van Slyke, found himself under suspicion for his handling of the sales.

The problems with bond sales were only the beginning, though. As banks failed in the East in 1857, the ripple effect spread rapidly west, and panic engulfed Wisconsin. Property values fell, city revenues dried up and city services and jobs were cut. Madison's most prominent citizen, Leonard Farwell, lost everything after failing to raise enough cash to stave off his creditors, sending shock waves throughout the city.[41] People, fearful for their futures, left Madison in droves. In just three years, Madison's population dropped by 40 percent.[42]

Perhaps worst of all, when the 1857 tax bill came, Madison taxpayers found themselves owing just as much as the year before, when times were good. The drop in city services had not reduced taxes because the city had spent nearly twice as much as it had budgeted.

Angry at the government's recklessness, taxpayers organized. They prepared written recommendations on how abuses by city officials could be prevented and offered suggestions on how the debt could be paid. The people called for deep reform, and unlike nearly all taxpayer demonstrations in history, they got their wish. In early February 1858, Governor Alexander Randall signed into law a charter amendment that imposed onerous mandates and fines for noncompliance and limited additional city funding to the $8,000 in the general fund.[43]

The depression also hurt the Watertown and Madison Railroad. Completed only to Waterloo by the time the depression hit, the line finally made it to Sun Prairie in 1859. That was far enough for some residents. Disgusted by the Milwaukee and Mississippi fares and service by this point, many Madison residents took the stagecoach to Sun Prairie to catch the line to Milwaukee.

Adding insult to injury was yet another attempt, in 1858, to move the capital from Madison to Milwaukee. Madison managed, once again, to hold on to its status, but not without considerable concern at the ease with which these removal efforts could muster support in the legislature.

Even in the midst of widespread suffering and devastation, Madison still saw some positive growth and change during the depression. Many workmen remained employed in state-funded construction projects, including the State Insane Asylum and Bascom Hall (then known as Main Hall) on the University of Wisconsin campus. Coal gaslight also made its first appearance in Madison in 1855. The Madison Gas Light and Coke Company received the exclusive franchise on the utility from the city, and within a few years, most city streets and many homes had gas lighting. Electric lights came in 1888. During this period, the construction of the Pierce House (1857), the Bashford House (1857), the Van Slyke House (1857), the Hoyt House (1858) and the Keenan House (1858) made Mansion Hill Madison's premier neighborhood. Three theaters, two private and one public, opened in 1858,[44] and a grand new city hall opened at the corner of West Mifflin Street and Wisconsin Avenue.

Construction had also begun on a new capitol building. After twenty years, the first Madison capitol had become inadequate to the growing needs of the state. In 1857, the legislature authorized the enlargement of the capitol and hired architects August Kutzbock and Samuel H. Donnel to complete the work. They decided on a phased replacement of the old capitol by building the new building around the old one to help minimize disruptions. Construction began in 1857 and continued until 1869, when the dome was finally completed. Two more wings were added on the north and south sides in the 1880s to house the State Historical Society of Wisconsin (which

Built in 1857, the Pierce House was the first residence in Madison's most elegant neighborhood, Mansion Hill. *Erika Janik.*

moved to its own building in 1900), the Supreme Court, the Wisconsin State Library and legislative staffs.

By 1860, the economic depression had become increasingly overshadowed by gathering clouds of war. When Abraham Lincoln's call for troops came in April 1861, most Madison residents believed that slavery was wrong and secession from the Union illegal. Seven years earlier, in 1854, Wisconsinites had helped to found Lincoln's party, the Republican Party, in Ripon, out of anger over the Kansas-Nebraska Act.

The act, introduced by Illinois senator Stephen A. Douglas, a Democrat, provided for the organization of the Kansas and Nebraska Territories, including the determination to leave the decision about slavery to the people and their elected officials. The act was a direct refutation of the 1820 Missouri Compromise, which had outlawed the extension of slavery to any new territories. Overnight, Kansas became a battleground for pro- and antislavery proponents. Perhaps more upsetting to Wisconsin residents, though, was the measure of the bill that denied noncitizen immigrants the right to vote or hold office in either territory, a personal affront to the thousands of noncitizen European immigrants who called Wisconsin home.

The Kansas-Nebraska Act provoked immediate outrage in Wisconsin. Anti-Kansas-Nebraska meetings were held throughout the country in the early months of 1854, including in Ripon, where, under the leadership of lawyer Alvan Bovay, representatives of various political groups suggested the formation of a new party, the Republican Party, to protest the bill.

On July 13, 1854, a convention was held on the lawn of the capitol in Madison to organize the new party. The members resolved, "That we accept this issue [freedom or slavery], forced upon us by the slave power, and in the defense of freedom will cooperate and be known as Republicans."[45] Made up of members of various political persuasions, leaders of the nascent party focused almost exclusively on the issue of slavery, largely because it was the single issue on which they all could agree.

Until the 1850s, most Wisconsin residents had taken little interest in slavery, though a few had become ardent abolitionists. Most of the state's antislavery leaders had migrated to villages in southeastern Wisconsin from New York and New England. Sympathy for fugitive slaves was common and grew in strength as the years passed. By the early 1840s, a few Wisconsin residents were denouncing slavery as morally wrong and began organizing to discuss what to do about it. A territorial antislavery society formed in June 1842 and, soon after, a branch of the New York–based antislavery Liberty Party. One year later, in 1843, sixteen-year-old Caroline Quarrls became the first slave to escape to Canada through Wisconsin.

An event in Racine in 1854 threw the slavery issue into the spotlight in Wisconsin. Missouri slave Joshua Glover had fled to Racine in 1854 seeking asylum. His master, upon learning his whereabouts, came to Wisconsin along with federal marshals and, under the federal Fugitive Slave Act of 1850, had Glover arrested and placed in the Milwaukee County Jail. Abolitionists from all over southeastern Wisconsin, led by local abolitionist editor Sherman Booth, surrounded the jail, broke down its doors and helped Glover escape safely to Canada.

For helping Glover, Booth was arrested on federal charges for violating the Fugitive Slave Act. Booth quickly became a cause célèbre among those who wished to free Wisconsin from any association with slavery. The Wisconsin Supreme Court ultimately vindicated Booth, declaring the Fugitive Slave Act unconstitutional on the basis of states' rights in 1855.

Madison newspapers became lively forums for debates over slavery and black equality more generally. The Democratic *Patriot* staked out an early opposition to black rights, claiming, beginning in 1856, that God and history showed blacks to be inferior to whites. The *Wisconsin State Journal* took the opposite tack under the pen of Republican Horace Rublee, printing numerous stories on the horrors of slavery in the South.

Although most Wisconsin residents disapproved of slavery, the right of black citizens to vote was another matter. In 1849, a majority of Wisconsin voters approved black suffrage, but voting rights were consistently denied to African Americans due to legal disputes over what constituted a "majority." An 1857 statewide referendum on black suffrage was rejected by a vote of five to one. African Americans did not receive the right to vote until 1866, when the Wisconsin Supreme Court weighed in on the matter.

The secession of South Carolina on December 20, 1860, led many, especially Republicans, to believe that conflict was inevitable. Governor Randall, in a stirring address to the legislature on January 10, 1861, proclaimed, "Secession is revolution, revolution is war and war against the government of the United States is treason."[46]

When the war finally broke out in April 1861, after the stunning fall of Fort Sumter, Wisconsin soldiers answered the call to duty and enlisted. On April 18, 1861, more than one thousand Madison residents gathered in the assembly chambers of the capitol and pledged more than $7,500 to support the families of volunteer soldiers. One farmer gave one hundred bushels of wheat. By the end of the war, Madison had raised more than $100,000 for soldiers and their families.[47]

Six days later, on April 24, practically the entire city turned out to send off Madison's citizen contribution to the war effort, two full-strength militia companies, the Governor's Guard and the Madison Guard. On the basis of population, Madison sent more than three times as many men as Milwaukee and twice as many as Fond du Lac. Janesville and Kenosha, much bigger cities than Madison, did not manage to organize a single company.[48]

Recruits were trained in Milwaukee, Fond du Lac, Racine and Madison. Camp Randall became Wisconsin's major training facility, located on fairgrounds about a mile and a half from the capitol. Attorney, editor and longtime Madison booster Horace A. Tenney was given the task of converting the thirty-acre fairgrounds into a military encampment, which was named in the governor's honor.

Work on the grounds had barely begun when the first troops arrived. Many thought that an elaborate camp was unnecessary since they believed

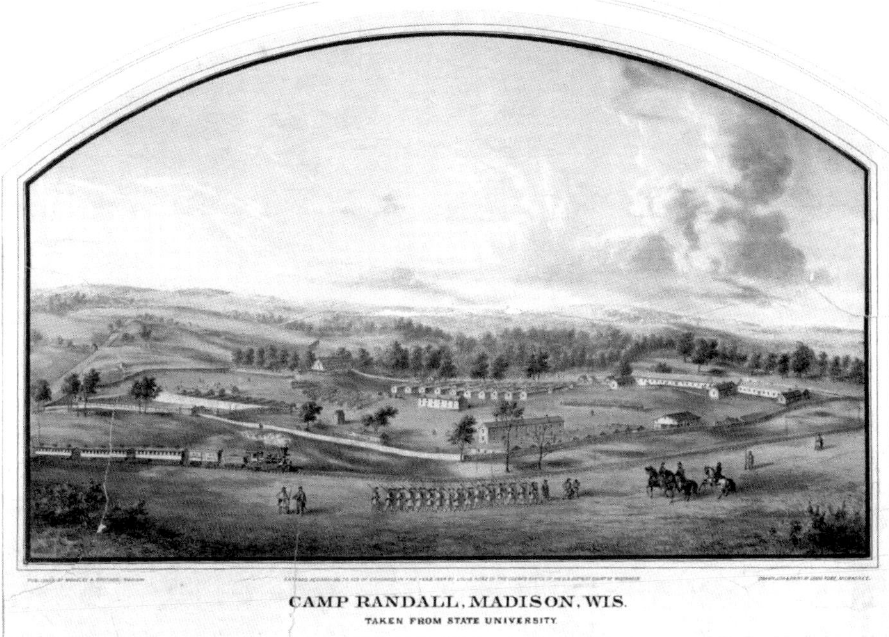

Camp Randall became a training camp for the Union during the Civil War. *Wisconsin Historical Society Image ID #1838.*

the war would be over quickly. They were wrong. By 1864, Camp Randall had become the state's largest and most important soldier-training complex, with ninety-four buildings capable of accommodating five thousand men at a time. When the war ended, seventy thousand of the nearly ninety-five thousand Wisconsin men who served had trained at Camp Randall.[49]

For enlisted men, a typical day at the camp began with roll call at 5:00 a.m. Breakfast was at 6:30 a.m., followed by several hours of free time until drill, which ran from 10:00 a.m. until noon. After lunch, the men were free until 2:00 p.m., when they would assemble for two hours of drills and regimental parades. Dinner was at 5:30 p.m. Most had nothing to do after dinner—or frankly, not all that much to do during their other free periods of the day.[50] Camp quickly became boring to the men, especially when all the attractions of a growing city—bars, dance halls, card games—were just a leap over the fence away. Thousands of young men gathered together in town with little to do inevitably led to problems.

The trouble began in June 1861, when several hundred men on furlough were set loose on Madison. One group allegedly killed a German woman, while another group of drunken soldiers tried to break into Voight's Brewery, exchanging gunfire with the patrons and proprietor, reported the *Daily Patriot*.

To address the problems, Mayor Levi Baker Vilas called a citizens meeting that nearly resulted in violence itself. The mayor then met with Colonel Coon, the commanding officer of the Second Regiment, to try to better enforce order among the men.

But over the next three years, soldiers continued to pose a threat to public order and safety. Merchants reported being beaten and robbed. Households complained of stolen turkeys and chickens. Drunken brawls broke out on city streets, and several assaults and attempted rapes were reported.

Blame for the problems fell, in part, on the poor conditions the men endured in camp. Soldiers complained of leaky roofs, rotten food and insect-infested clothing and bedding. Newspaper reports of protests and riots over the poor conditions became a staple of Camp Randall life. A U.S. Senate investigation of camp conditions in late 1862 and early 1863 found that the men were not exaggerating. The committee report published in the 1863 *Senate Journal* describes cattle sheds "wholly unfit for any human being to live in," beans "in a state of decay and entirely unfit for use" and coffee "so unsavory and deleterious as to be beyond use." Although camp officials countered that conditions were not as bad as reported, numerous improvements to the camp were immediately ordered.

Besides training and housing Union soldiers, Camp Randall also became a prison for more than 1,000 Confederate soldiers. Some managed to escape, but close to 150 died and were buried at Forest Hill Cemetery.

Already strained relations between the city and camp grew more so in late 1863, when Lincoln called for an additional 600,000 men. His call included a federal draft system to ensure results, an addition that taught Madison residents the difference between soldiers there by choice and those there by force. The first draftees began arriving at Camp Randall in February 1864. By late April, more than 3,000 soldiers lived at Camp Randall, nearly one soldier for every three citizens.

Despite strict rules and precautions, the resourceful soldiers still managed to bring a reign of terror to Madison within weeks of their arrival. A violent confrontation broke out between citizens and soldiers at Sprecher Brewery in May 1864. The first murder happened in June, followed by a second just two months later. Assault, battery and robbery once again became daily occurrences. Neither the military nor city authorities were able to stop the violence until the war's end.

War created work and affected the lives of everyone, regardless of whether they became part of the Union effort. Wisconsin women mostly stayed home but literally picked up the reins that their fathers, husbands and brothers had dropped. Women formed ladies' aid societies to care for the families of soldiers, many left destitute by the loss of male laborers. They collected and distributed food, clothing and wood. Women also organized to make uniforms and bandages.[51]

One Madison woman, Cordelia Harvey, widow of Wisconsin governor Louis P. Harvey, who had tragically drowned while inspecting Wisconsin troops, organized charitable activities and arranged for the transfer of many wounded soldiers to Northern hospitals. After visiting hospitals throughout the South, Harvey became convinced that only the cooler Northern climate would restore Wisconsin soldiers to health. After repeated visits to Washington to meet with War Secretary Edwin Stanton and President Lincoln himself, Harvey got her wish. The Harvey United States Army General Hospital opened in October 1863 in the grand house once owned by Leonard Farwell. One year later, a new wing increased the hospital's capacity to six hundred patients. So many men were sent to the Harvey Hospital that the overflow had to be accommodated at the Camp Randall infirmary. The hospital closed in September 1865.

After the hospital closed, Harvey led the effort to convert the building into a school for the children of soldiers killed in service. Opened in 1866, the school taught more than 650 children in its nine years of operation

Wisconsin's economy, barely recovered from the 1857 depression when the war began, managed wartime fairly well. After several poor seasons, in 1860 farmers produced a bumper crop of wheat, which led the recovery of Madison's economy.[52] Nearly a third of Wisconsin banks failed in 1861, largely due to their heavy investment in Southern bonds. But a strong pact not to accept the notes of weaker Wisconsin banks, an agreement all Madison banks were part of, spared Madison residents the devastation suffered by others.[53]

Manufacturing grew on the strength of agricultural implements, the city's leading industry by 1864. Madison's leading manufacturer was the E.W. Skinner Company, which specialized in reapers and mowers. In 1861, Skinner began making sorghum mills, as Madison briefly became the center of Wisconsin's sorghum industry.[54] Manufacturing was further encouraged by the absence of such Southern crops as cotton and sugar. Acreage devoted to cotton substitutes like wool and flax increased dramatically.

Madison finally got its second railroad, too, when the Chicago and Northwestern Railroad steamed into town in September 1864. The new line finally ended the decade-long monopoly by the Milwaukee and Prairie du Chien.

News of General Lee's surrender at Appomattox reached Madison on the evening of April 9, 1865. The governor ordered a gun salute at the capitol, and soon bells all over the city joined in the ringing celebration.

Trainloads of returning soldiers began arriving in town in June and July 1865. Madison residents greeted the trains with cheers, and some units received extravagant meals compliments of the state.[55] Of the 722 Madison men who went to war, 171 did not make it back.[56]

Soon after the war ended, nearly every sign of Madison's role as a wartime camp was gone. Most of the buildings at Camp Randall had been torn down and sold for scrap lumber. The liveliness of the camp, with its colorful parades and martial band music, was gone. Gone, too, was the rowdiness that had terrorized citizens for nearly four years. Most Madison residents were only too happy to have their town back.[57]

7

CALLING MADISON HOME

"The natural resources of Wisconsin are almost unlimited and nothing is wanted but the hand of cultivation to make it the garden of the world," wrote Albert G. Tuttle in a letter to his wife back home in Connecticut. "There is a softness and beauty in the landscape which is indescribable and which the hand of art will fail to improve."

Tuttle had come west to investigate Wisconsin for a possible move in the 1840s, traveling through much of southern Wisconsin, including Madison. And despite facing down a wolf while traveling the shores of Lake Monona, Tuttle still wrote home a glowing report of his trip, which was later reprinted in the *Baraboo Republic* newspaper.[58] Described in such flattering terms, how could anyone resist moving to Wisconsin?

Many could not. Between 1836 and 1860, people flooded into Wisconsin. Some of these settlers came from the eastern United States, but an increasing number came from Europe. Economic and social changes in Europe, coupled with natural disasters such as the potato blight in Ireland, pushed many Europeans to emigrate.

Between 1852 and 1855, the Wisconsin Commission of Emigration, created by Madison promoter and governor Leonard Farwell, actively encouraged the settlement of European immigrants. Immigrants were seen as the fuel for the state's growth. The commission published pamphlets praising the state's virtues in the German, Norwegian, Dutch and English languages and distributed them throughout Europe and in eastern U.S. port cities to encourage people to come west.

Not everyone was so happy about all the new foreign faces, however. Yankees had long dominated the Wisconsin frontier, partly because they knew the mechanics of U.S. land surveys and sales and often had a line of credit to get them started. They took early possession of town sites, water power and some of the best farmlands, and they became the entrepreneurs, speculators, lawyers, editors, ministers and leading politicians. Madison's earliest settlers were no different than those in the rest of the state, being young and usually Yankees from New England and New York.

That all changed in the 1850s with increasing immigration. As a result, Madison's population boomed, growing by 1,500 percent and bringing profound changes to the character of the city. Between 1850 and 1855, Madison went from a predominantly native-born population to one dominated by immigrants. Where 60 percent of Madison residents were American born in 1850, more than half were foreign born or the children of immigrants just five years later.[59] Many among the Yankee population did not respond well to the changes.

Newspapers derided the new arrivals, and the nativist, or Know-Nothing, movement that had taken hold nationally found eager adherents in Madison. Members strongly opposed immigrants, especially those who were followers of the Catholic Church, and worked to keep immigrants from holding public office and finding jobs. They called themselves Know-Nothings because it was a secret organization; when asked, followers often said that they "knew nothing" about it. Elisha Keyes reported that many of those who attended the Republican convention in Madison in 1855 were actually Know-Nothings "masquerading under the name Republican."[60] Whatever personal aversion to immigrants they might have felt, however, most Madison merchants and politicians still sought immigrant dollars and votes: the constituency was becoming simply too large to ignore.

The Sabbath day proved the greatest source of tension between Yankees and immigrants. Abstemious Yankees believed that Sundays should be spent going to church and reading the Bible, nothing else. German immigrants, on the other hand, took a more liberal view and argued that Sundays were for having fun with friends, drinking, dancing and playing games. Condemned at first for their behavior, some Yankees later came to accept, and in some cases, even advocate, for the German model of Sunday celebration. "There are many of the social habits of our adopted citizens that would be profitable for us to imitate," wrote Beriah Brown, editor of the *Daily Argus and Democrat*. "Americans seem to enter upon every undertaking with so much gravity that they make their holidays dull affairs."[61]

Not every immigrant group was unwelcome, however. English immigrants received the warmest reception, largely because they were not all that different from the Yankees, save for their accent. Despite speaking English, the Irish did not enjoy the same favorable treatment and were often viewed with disdain for their Catholic faith and drinking habits. Of the non-English speakers, the Norwegians, with their Protestantism, strong work ethic and sober temperaments, were the most popular.[62]

Yankees continued to control a disproportionate share of local power and resources, despite composing only 20 to 25 percent of the population in the 1870s. Called Madison's "codfish aristocracy" by the *Wisconsin State Journal* (cod being a saltwater fish common to the Atlantic), this elite group lived in the finest homes in the best neighborhoods.[63] They held the highest-paid jobs in white-collar professions and took leading roles in starting and promoting Madison's intellectual activities and organizations. They also maintained a tight grip on the mayor's office. Between 1865 and 1880, nine of the city's twelve mayors were either born in New England or were the children of parents from New England or New York.[64]

As Madison's foreign population grew after the Civil War, so did its influence. Germans were the largest ethnic group, followed by the Norwegians and the Irish. The German immigrants, in particular, exerted a large influence on the city. They started their own churches and began Madison's first kindergarten program in 1879. All five of Madison breweries—Fauerbach, Hausmann, Brechheimer, Rodermund and Mautz-Hess—were owned by Germans. German enthusiasm for riflery led to the formation of the Madison Schuetzen Club, a shooting club for men to practice their marksmanship. The Germans also heavily contributed to the Democratic Party, so much so that the Republicans launched their own Turnverien, a German athletic and social club, to try to win over German voters.[65]

Madison's Norwegians contributed their share of intellectual and cultural institutions as well. The old Soldiers Orphans Home that Cordelia Harvey started after the Civil War became the principal seminary for the Norwegian Lutheran Synod and a high school for wealthy Norwegians who wanted their children to receive a strongly religious education in the 1870s.[66] Norwegians

Benedict Goldenberger and his family were just some of the German Americans who called Madison home. *Wisconsin Historical Society Image ID #1971.*

also introduced a new holiday to the Wisconsin calendar when they began celebrating Norwegian Independence Day, *Syttende Mai*, in the mid-1870s with a parade and party.[67]

The city's oldest inhabitants, the Ho-Chunk, still lived in Madison, too. Although the U.S. government officially banished the Ho-Chunk from Madison in 1833, many continued to live in and near the city. Mills Woods (now Elmside Boulevard), Fullers Woods (now Maple Bluff), Frost Woods (now the city of Monona) and the University of Wisconsin Arboretum were some of the favored Ho-Chunk campsites in the late nineteenth century. A few sold mink and muskrat pelts on the Capitol Square to make money. While most whites treated the Ho-Chunk with only a strained acceptance, one man, archaeologist Charles E. Brown, befriended area Indians and helped to preserve their history and legends.

The city's population stagnated in the late nineteenth century, growing at just 3 percent between 1880 and 1895. The flat growth rate frustrated city officials, who struggled to find the key, be it manufacturing, the university or something else, to drive growth and expansion.

Finally, in 1895, Madison's population began to grow at a rate to match the hopes of those who sought to boom the city. The new residents, mostly immigrants, had a difficult time, however. The Yankees continued to hold tight to the upper crust of Madison society, despite being grossly outnumbered by immigrants. They owned most of the banks and most of the city property. Most immigrants were forced to work lower-paying and lower-status jobs.

This began to change in the early twentieth century, however. Most immigrants sent their children to public schools, where they learned English and developed strong attachments to their adopted country. Shut out of many professions, some immigrants established their own businesses and became part of the city's business community. Madison's leading manufacturer was Norwegian immigrant John A. Johnson, whose implement factory and machine shop became the city's largest employer. Madison also elected its first foreign mayor in 1897: Matthew Hoven, the first German and first Catholic to hold the position.

The growing power of immigrants did not always sit well with the establishment Yankees. Newspapers continued to treat them poorly, publishing many anonymous letters to the editor urging immigrants to go home. Many officials tried to close saloons on Sundays, too, an easy way to enrage the German community.

Italians were one of the new immigrant groups to come to Madison in the early twentieth century. Ten Italian men came up to Madison from Chicago to work on the railroad. Writing home to relatives, the men reported that Madison had abundant food, jobs and opportunities, conditions that seemed impossible to imagine back home in Sicily. At the time, disease, overcrowding and poverty plagued the island, and the Italian government had begun encouraging emigration as a way of relieving population pressures. The combination of free passports, cheap transatlantic steamship tickets and the promise of a better life in America led to massive Italian migration around the turn of the twentieth century.

The Italians who came to Madison settled in the Greenbush, or the Bush, neighborhood, an area bounded by Brooks, West Washington and Regent Streets. The area was also popular with Eastern European Jews and blacks. The neighborhood, constructed largely on top of a trash-filled marsh, soon became Madison's first slum. Developers built cheap homes to shelter Madison's poorest residents, many of whom crowded whole families into single rooms. More than half of the homes came from other parts of the city, disassembled and hastily rebuilt in the Bush.[68] One-third of the homes had no running water, and many residents had to travel more than a block to find a water source.[69] To make matters worse, the marshy land beneath the homes sometimes flooded, filling the neighborhood with stagnant, disease-breeding water. The city did nothing to help.

Regarded with contempt by middle- and upper-class residents for their peasant background and inability to speak English, Madison's Italians quickly formed a tightknit community with their own stores, organizations and church. Italian men often had a difficult time supporting their families. With little English and few job skills, most could scarcely offer employers more than their physical labor, so they became Madison's ditch diggers, quarry workers and construction workers. By 1916, Madison's "Little Italy" had more than one thousand residents, becoming, by 1920, Madison's third-largest immigrant group.

Russian and German Jews who came to Madison around 1900 also faced their share of obstacles. Impoverished, they, too, settled in the Bush because it offered affordable housing and a more tolerant atmosphere than other Madison neighborhoods.[70] Like the Italians, they worked unskilled jobs and formed a tight community united by religion and ethnicity. They built the Aguda Achim Synagogue at Park and Mound Streets in 1904 and the Beth Israel Synagogue in 1934.[71]

The Greenbush neighborhood was also popular with Madison's small black community, as many landlords in other parts of the city refused to rent to them. The redevelopment of the neighborhood in the 1960s forced many African Americans to South Madison.

From the late nineteenth century through the end of World War II, immigration policy in the United States underwent dramatic changes that helped to alter both the pace and the face of immigration. High rates of immigration in the nineteenth century had sparked nativist sentiment and encouraged the introduction of restrictive federal legislation, particularly toward Asian immigrants. Madison's small Chinese community was continually victimized by prejudice and overt attacks on their businesses, including a confederation of white steam laundries that assailed Chinese-owned laundries as dirty and unsafe.

The 1965 Immigration and Nationality Act removed restrictions based on national origins in favor of a preference system that gave priority to family reunification and political refugees. This act particularly helped bring Hmong refugees from Laos to Wisconsin, and to Madison, in large numbers in the 1970s and 1980s.

Recruited to serve as guerilla soldiers during the Vietnam War, the Hmong lived in the crossfire during the war. When the United States withdrew from Vietnam in 1975, the Hmong who had aided the Americans were left in the hands of the communists they had fought against. Thousands fled to refugee camps in Thailand, where resettlement organizations, such as the U.S. Catholic Conference and Lutheran Immigration and Refugee Services, helped to sponsor Hmong immigration to the United States.

Like other immigrants, Hmong refugees faced many challenges adjusting to American culture, particularly racist and prejudicial attitudes. Many state and community organizations attempted to educate Wisconsinsites on Hmong culture and the Hmong on American culture. Madison was home to more than eighteen hundred Hmong immigrants in 2000.

Although Hispanics have lived in Wisconsin since before statehood, they did not become a sizable population until the 1950s. Prior to the 1950s, most

Hmong are some of Madison's newest immigrants. Many sell produce at area farmers' markets. *Erika Janik.*

Mexicans in Wisconsin were migrant laborers recruited by manufacturers and agricultural contractors to fill labor shortages. Mexicans are today the largest Spanish-speaking group in Wisconsin, along with sizable populations from Puerto Rico, Cuba, El Salvador, Colombia and Nicaragua.

Established in 1983, Centro Hispano began providing language and other services to Cuban refugees who had settled in Madison. As the Hispanic population grew, Centro expanded its services to help more immigrants integrate into their adopted community. In 2000, Dane County had more than fourteen thousand Hispanic residents.

From its singular origins as largely white and Yankee, Madison has become remarkably diverse for its size and location in the upper Midwest. Asians and Hispanics are among the city's fastest-growing immigrant groups, and a look at the world café of restaurants lining State Street illustrates how many different peoples now call Madison home.

8

LEARNING HOW TO RELAX

Although people have always enjoyed some type of recreation and fun, leisure and vacation time were relative luxuries in a frontier community like Madison, particularly among the middle and lower classes. Until the middle of the nineteenth century, Americans used the word vacation the way the English did, to signify a time when teachers and students "vacate" their schools and go off on their own, usually to work at home. Leisure was a privilege for the wealthy or an occasional reward for hard work rather than a right in and of itself. Only the weekly Sabbath day, which already had a specific purpose, broke up the daily struggle for food, shelter and clothing. And in Wisconsin, even this day caused conflict between the sober Yankee settlers and the fun-loving Catholic immigrants.

Over time, the idea of vacation and weekend leisure time became more widely available and enjoyed. What Madison residents did for fun depended in large part on the state of the economy, personal wealth and, this being Wisconsin, the season. For much of Madison's early years, residents sought simple, inexpensive pastimes, such as parties in homes, boating and watching the legislature (yes, this qualified as entertainment in the nineteenth century). In the winter, ice-skating, sledding and iceboating made the long season more fun.

The first major entertainment event held in Madison was Wisconsin's first state fair in September 1858. Among the fair's most popular entertainments was the competition between fire companies to see which one could climb rope ladders most quickly. Participants also enjoyed garden projects, floral displays, minstrel performances, plays and carnival-like sideshows. The fair returned to Madison in 1860 and 1861, and to keep it in Madison, city leaders levied a tax to improve the grounds and structures. The Civil War interrupted the annual fair, however, as the state fairgrounds, now much improved with taxpayer dollars, became the soldier training center known as Camp Randall.[72]

Madison's entertainment scene improved after the Civil War, due in no small part to the increasing number of immigrants settling in Madison. German choirs, such as the Maennerchor, an all-male choir, and the Liederkranz Society, a mixed choir, along with German bands, became integral forms of community entertainment that helped to increase popular appreciation of classical music. The Madison Turnverein, founded by German immigrants in 1855, hosted plays, concerts and singing festivals, in addition to physical acrobatics. (The word *Turnverein* comes from the German *turnen*, "to do gymnastics," and *verein*, "club.") Eventually, nearly all of Madison's German organizations and groups became associated with the Turnverein.

In the 1870s, famed Norwegian violinist Ole Borneman Bull came to call Madison his American home. Bull had made his name in Europe as a concert violinist before he arrived for the first of what would be many North American concert tours in 1843. By the 1870s, after several decades of extended tours, Bull had become one of the most popular performers in America and a popular symbol of Norwegian culture.

At an appearance in Madison in 1868, Bull met his future wife, Madison resident Sara Thorp. They married two years later and spent the next nine years in Madison; that is, when Bull was not on tour or visiting his Norwegian estate. Bull also became good friends with University of Wisconsin Norwegian instructor Rasmus B. Anderson, and he played many benefit concerts to raise money for Anderson's new Scandinavian Studies Department. With Bull's help, Madison became a center for the study of Norse culture. Bull left Madison in 1879, dying the following year at his Norwegian island home.[73]

The opening of the Hooley Opera House in 1871 dramatically improved Madison's theatrical and performance spaces. Before 1871, stock and repertory theater companies had dominated the city playbills. The opening of the opera house brought more traveling companies with well-known stars in dramas, comedies and musicals.[74] The Hooley also brought more cultured entertainment than ever before, including Shakespearean dramas,

Ole Bull once lived in this house, which has also served as the governor's mansion and, since the 1950s, as a residential community for University of Wisconsin graduate students. *Erika Janik.*

symphonies and instrumental groups. Even so, the most popular shows that filled the Hooley were entertainers like Buffalo Bill. Madison residents loved minstrel shows, too, with their ethnic humor that often denigrated the Chinese and African Americans. The shows were so well received that the city soon supported two local minstrel groups, in addition to the traveling shows.[75] Unfortunately, a water leak from the adjoining Turkish bath forced the Hooley to close in 1885, creating a void in the city's entertainment scene.

Madison got a new theater in 1890 with the opening of the Fuller Opera House. Built by Morris E. Fuller and his son Edward, the Fuller became Madison's first great theater, hosting everything from vaudeville acts to symphony orchestras several times a week. Unfortunately, the Fuller was not a financial success, and in 1921, it was remodeled into the Parkway movie theater.[76]

Despite being surrounded by water, Madison residents did not take full advantage of the recreational opportunities afforded by the lakes until the late nineteenth century. Many residents had boats, but most were primitive dugouts. In July 1870, Madison held its first sailing regatta, an event that

The Fuller Opera House filled a void in Madison's entertainment scene when it opened in 1890, playing host to everything from vaudeville to orchestras. *Wisconsin Historical Society Image ID #11208.*

proved so popular that four more were held that summer. The following year, the Madison Yacht Club was organized.[77] Around the same time, rowing became increasingly popular, and the Monona Rowing Club formed in the spring of 1870.[78] The establishment of regular steamboat service on Lake Mendota and Lake Monona in the late 1870s made Madison's lakes more accessible to residents and visitors than ever before.

Part of the city's slow embrace of its lakes may have resulted from the city's ban on swimming. In 1851, the village of Madison banned swimming and bathing in the public view in Lake Monona and Lake Mendota between 5:00 a.m. and 9:00 p.m. The city adopted nearly the same ordinance in 1856 but expanded the prohibited area to within one mile from the shore.[79] The prohibition of swimming was far from popular, however, and after several boys were arrested for skinny-dipping, the city legalized swimming in 1879, provided the swimmers wore bathing suits that covered them from neck to knee.[80]

The University of Wisconsin (UW) brought organized sports to Madison for the first time in the late nineteenth century. Football was introduced in 1890 and quickly became Madison's most popular spectator sport. Some games drew as many as ten thousand people to Camp Randall, the Civil War training camp cum football field that the university purchased in 1893. The university also fielded teams in tennis, track and field, basketball and baseball.

The UW's baseball team was not Madison's first team. High school students and other city men organized Madison's first baseball game in 1860 on a vacant lot on the corner of Gorham Street and Wisconsin Avenue. The Civil War interrupted play, but as soon as the war ended, baseball became a virtual obsession. Part of baseball's appeal was its low cost—all you needed was a bat and ball to play. The pages of the *Wisconsin State Journal* were filled with recaps of games played by Madison teams against teams from across Wisconsin, as well as states farther afield in the late 1860s.[81]

In the late nineteenth century, Madison residents eagerly embraced a new form of transportation and fun: the bicycle. The French velocipede first captured the public imagination in the 1860s. With a springless seat and a frame weighing in at 150 pounds, riders often called them "boneshakers" for the jarring and difficult-to-balance ride they offered. Nonetheless, several Madison residents purchased them. The elegant high-wheeled bike was the next to appear in Madison in the 1880s. The high front wheel made these new bikes faster and easier to maneuver than the velocipede, but they also shifted a rider's center of gravity, making them incredibly dangerous to ride.

The introduction of the safety wheel bicycle in the late 1880s, with its soft and equally sized tires, created a bicycling craze in Madison. Rides around Lake Monona and on Lake Mendota Drive became favorite weekend activities. Part of what made bicycling so popular was that unlike other sports, both men and women could enjoy it. Bicycling also offered a cheap and convenient way for men and women to get to and from work.[82]

By the turn of the twentieth century, Madison residents enjoyed a rich selection of plays, concerts and vaudeville shows. But the heyday of the live, traveling performance company was drawing to a close as a new form of entertainment swept the country.

Madison's first movie theater opened on State Street in January 1909. The Grand proved an immediate hit, as employees turned customers away night after night for nearly a year.[83] Four years later, Madison had eight new or remodeled theaters showing movies. In its 1915 recreational survey of residents, the Madison Board of Commerce found that one in five residents went to the movies each Sunday. Some residents were even more die-hard movie fans; the *Wisconsin State Journal* reported in 1913 that one in ten residents attended a movie each day. Madison got its first grand movie palace in 1918 with the opening of the fifteen-hundred-seat Strand Theater.

Radio made its Madison debut in the late teens. In 1919, two radio stations, 9XM and WIBA, went on the air, and residents began purchasing or making radios to pick up the broadcasts for in-home entertainment. 9XM radio, today's Wisconsin Public Radio, began regularly scheduled programming in 1921, the first in the nation. It also became the first station to give a weather forecast and the first to broadcast a live symphony concert. 9XM became WHA in 1922, relicensed by the U.S Commerce Department as one of the first educational radio stations in the country.[84]

The development of entertainment venues and outlets in Madison's first decades set the stage for future growth. Once residents discovered all that the world had to offer in music, art, theater and sports, as well as the recreational opportunities in their own backyard, Madison never looked back.

9

CHURCHES, SCHOOLS AND NEWSPAPERS

In Madison's early years, like in many frontier towns, most of the money generated through land sales and trade was directed toward construction projects and land investment, leaving few resources dedicated to cultural and intellectual pursuits. Many settlers and visitors from the East found the American frontier (which, coincidentally, ran nearly straight through Madison in 1840 according to the U.S. Census) culturally repugnant. Englishman Dr. Goodhue visited Madison with his friend General John A. Brown in 1842. After several days spent tramping around in foul weather past drunks sleeping in the mud and crude buildings, Dr. Goodhue exclaimed, "John A.! If you tell anybody that I *ever was in Madison*, by God I'll kill you!"[85]

If still little more than a frontier village, Madison was not without its cultural improvements by the mid-1840s. Madison could boast one church, one schoolhouse and three newspapers, all in its first decade.

Madison's first formal religious service occurred during the summer of 1837. A Methodist minister from Illinois rode into town and offered to preach, a proposal residents eagerly accepted.[86] That a Methodist arrived first was not surprising. Methodist ministers often reached frontier communities first, spreading their faith by the circuit rider and the revival meeting and winning converts by closely following the line of settlement west.

Circuit riders and missionaries provided most religious services in early Madison. The American Home Missionary Society, a national organization dedicated to establishing Christianity in the West, established an official mission outpost in Madison, the capital of Wisconsin, and sent Reverend Slingerland to serve. He presided at the founding of the First Congregational Church in October 1840.[87] The Episcopalians followed a similar path, declaring Madison an official mission outpost and sending a missionary to establish a church. Grace Episcopal Church opened on March 4, 1840.[88]

Church memberships were small, and most denominations did not have their own church buildings, so many met in homes, stores and even in the capitol building. Some denominations held services in the capitol for years. Madison finally got its first official church building in 1846, a plain building on Webster Street owned by the First Congregational Church.[89]

As Madison's immigrant population grew, so did the number and kinds of churches. German immigrants established St. Paul's Presbyterian Church, the German Methodist Church, St. John's Lutheran Church, the German Evangelical Church, Holy Redeemer Catholic Church and the Shaare Schomaim Synagogue. In 1866, six of Madison's eleven churches conducted services in German.[90]

Difficult economic times in the mid-nineteenth century prevented many churches from raising enough money to fund the construction of a building.

The Gates of Heaven Synagogue was built in 1863 and is one of the oldest-surviving synagogue buildings in the country. *Erika Janik.*

Brief economic recoveries did allow some churches to improve existing structures or to build new larger, fancier buildings.[91] Most of these churches were located downtown and served the wealthier members of the city.

But as the city grew, much of that growth occurred away from downtown, making it difficult for downtown churches to attract new members. Several denominations decided to reach out to the unchurched by introducing Sunday schools. Inspired by British models, most American Sunday schools existed to educate the poor, writes historian Anne M. Boylan in *Sunday School*. These schools became more evangelistic in the mid-nineteenth century, existing for the primary purpose of reaching out and assimilating new people into the church. Nearly all of Madison churches offered Sunday school by the 1870s.

Madison churches also stopped expecting residents to come to them and began taking their churches to the people by establishing suburban branches. The Congregationalists remodeled an old schoolhouse at the corner of Brearly and Jenifer Streets into the Sixth Ward Chapel. The chapel was an outgrowth of the Sunday school that had formed at the Soldiers' Orphans' Home after the Civil War.[92] The Methodists took a different tack, setting up a huge tent in the summer of 1895 with seating for five hundred near the intersection of Williamson and Baldwin Streets for revivals.[93] Competing with both groups was the Salvation Army, which took its attention-grabbing musical instruments and songs to the streets to win converts.[94]

Schools were another uphill battle against frontier conditions. Many of the New Englanders among Wisconsin's white settlers were shocked at the condition of schools in their new home and ardently supported the creation of a public education system. Teachers were scarce, though, and those few were often fresh out of school themselves, instructing several grades at once in crowded schoolhouses.

A log cabin on the corner of King and East Doty became the site of Madison's first school in 1838. Led by a twenty-two-year-old teacher, the dozen students attended a term that lasted only from March through May. Madison got its first regular schoolhouse one year later, in 1839, near the corner of East Johnson and Pinckney Streets. Within five years, the school was busting at its seams with fifty students packed inside the eighteen- by twenty-foot building.[95]

The school was replaced with a brick building on the corner of East Washington and South Butler in 1845. It, too, was almost immediately outgrown, with one hundred students packed into its two rooms by the spring of 1846.

With no room in the public schools, some Madison parents sent their children to private schools. Most of these private schools did not last long, though, as they were unable to support themselves on the low fees they could charge to people in a small frontier village. Until Wisconsin became a state, financial support for territorial schools could come only through taxes, and many citizens fought hard against high taxation rates. It took time to convince people of the necessity of voluntary taxation to educate other people's children as well as their own.

Ten years after it was built, the 1845 brick schoolhouse was still the only school in Madison, stuffed to its gills and barely serving the more than 1,600 school-aged children. Those who could not fit inside were sent to makeshift classrooms in churches and a carriage factory. Teachers remained so scarce (in part because they were so underpaid and sometimes not paid at all) that students faced a teacher-student ratio of nearly 1 to 125.[96]

When Wisconsin became a state in 1848, the new constitution provided for something few other states had: a state university and a system of free common schools. Funded by taxes and land sales, these schools made education widely available for all children between the ages of four and twenty. However, limited resources constrained much school improvement statewide until after the Civil War.

A new era in Madison schools began with the arrival of Damon Kilgore in April 1854. A twenty-seven-year-old Methodist minister, Kilgore arrived in town not to preach but to teach. But he was shocked by what he found: a community of five thousand people and fifteen hundred children but only one school with room for fewer than fifty students.[97] Indignant at the poor conditions but eager to help, Kilgore set right to work improving the city's schools.

For his first act, Kilgore convinced the legislature to create a Madison Board of Education and got himself appointed the first superintendent of schools. From this post, he vigorously campaigned to convince Madison citizens to support education and public schools. Kilgore, a disciple of famed educator Horace Mann, invited Mann to Madison to lecture on the evils of ignorance to help make his case. He also held parents responsible for their children's absences from school and worked with teachers to improve the quality of instruction in the classroom.[98]

At the same time, Kilgore tried to get public officials to set aside money for schools and school equipment. The village board proved unwilling to work with him, though; it was more interested in land speculation and keeping taxes down.[99] He had more success in 1856, when Madison became a city, though the city's extreme financial difficulties in 1857–58 drastically cut teachers' pay and resulted in only two of four schoolhouses being built. Kilgore continued to push for more school buildings and finally succeeded in convincing the board of education to purchase a high school, the former Madison Female Academy, in 1858. He also rented facilities in outlying areas of the city for schools.[100]

When Kilgore left Madison in 1860 to become principal of the Evansville Seminary, the city's public schools were dramatically changed.[101] From one school in 1854, Madison now boasted two new elementary schools and a high school. Kilgore introduced a graded school system and a curriculum that included music and exercise, and he trained a central group of teachers to be more effective instructors. Most importantly, he helped bolster community support for public education.

Public education remained inadequately funded after Kilgore left, and schools continued to be crowded. Not until after the Civil War did public schools receive a strong financial commitment from the city.

Between 1865 and 1880, despite serious financial limitations, Madison officials pumped one out of every four dollars into schools.[102] The city built its first new public high school in 1873, a source of much pride as the capstone of the city's educational system. The building boom meant that for the first time, Madison schools had more seats than enrolled students.[103]

Funding for schools improved when women received the right to vote in any election "pertaining to school matters" in 1884. Women played an active role in the movement to improve public schools in the nineteenth century, a role deemed acceptable to many male policy makers who otherwise wanted to keep women out of government decisions. Thanks to the widespread support of the city's women, a new high school opened in downtown Madison in 1908 on Gorham Street. The school was demolished in 1986, but its Oxfordian-style arch remains outside what is today the downtown campus of the Madison Area Technical College.

Although a university had been proposed in 1836, not until Wisconsin's Constitutional Convention of 1847 did the idea receive serious attention and consideration. The convention included a specific provision for the

The arch is all that remains of Madison Central High School, which opened its doors in 1908. *Erika Janik.*

establishment of a state university "at or near the seat of government" and called for the formation of a board of regents to govern the school. A few months after Wisconsin became the thirtieth state, the board of regents appointed a committee to negotiate the purchase of the land that had been known as College Hill ever since 1838. The legislature approved the purchase of 157 acres in 1849.

The University of Wisconsin actually began operation somewhere else, though. From February 1849 through 1851, the university used the Madison Women's Seminary on the corner of Wisconsin Avenue and East Johnson as its "preparatory department." There, Professor John Sterling taught seventeen boys, most from Madison, advanced skills to prepare them for university-level work. This rented building served as the university until North Hall opened in 1851.

The university grew slowly at first. From 1865 to 1885, the student population fluctuated from three hundred to five hundred. But in the last decade of the nineteenth century, the university expanded rapidly and came to exert a much greater influence on Madison. Between 1887 and 1900, the university's population quadrupled to 2,000 students. The faculty also grew

University of Wisconsin students on the lawn of Main Hall, later known as Bascom Hall, in 1869. *Wisconsin Historical Society Image ID #27716.*

from 40 employees in 1887 to 113 in 1896. Nearly 1 in every 10 Madison residents was a UW student or faculty member by 1900.[104]

To provide for this rapidly expanding student population, the university began a major building program between 1887 and 1900. Among the buildings constructed were some of the university's most iconic structures: Science Hall (1887), Hiram Smith Hall (1891), Red Gym (1893), Camp Randall grandstand (1896), the Dairy Barn (1897), the Education Building (1899) and the State Historical Society (1899). Of these, Hiram Smith Hall made a significant splash, housing the first permanent dairy instructional course in the western hemisphere. The course was developed in response to agricultural chemist Stephen Babcock's butterfat tester, which won him wide acclaim and helped to stimulate the dairy industry in Wisconsin.

The growth of the university delighted city leaders and many citizens who hoped it would encourage others to view Madison as a major educational center. The university helped promote a community ethos that valued intellectualism, the arts and literature—"the hum of culture," as one resident put it.[105] It also forced business leaders to see the university as a powerful source of economic growth and one worth supporting.

As it grew, the university began to permeate all aspects of the city, including city politics. Efforts to reform city government received strong support from the university, and several professors were elected to the common council. Professors also provided advice and specialized expertise on city problems.

While some thought the university had too much influence, most felt that it only made the city better. Moreover, the presence of the university served to increase community appreciation for public education and caused citizens to pay more attention to all of the city's schools.

Libraries were slower to appear in Madison than schools. Madison's first public library, the Madison Free Library, opened in two rooms on the second floor of the city hall in 1875, with Virginia Robbins as the city's first librarian. Opening with a little more than three thousand volumes, residents were invited to bring a book to donate to the city collection. Initially, children under the age of fifteen were not allowed inside, though their parents could check out books for them. Patrons dropped beans into boxes labeled history, literature, religion, travel, fiction and science when they checked out a book so Robbins could keep track of the number and types of books borrowed.

The Madison Free Library's board of directors took an extremely active and highly controlling role in the library's function. It created and enforced library rules, selected and arranged the books and oversaw all major library operations. To its governing board, the library provided a tremendous public service by teaching citizens about American culture and helping citizens improve their morals and intellect. The library also helped citizens spend their time wisely. "There are two very important objects to be steadily kept in view in a properly organized and conducted free library," read the *Fourth Annual Report of the Board of Directors of the Free Library and Reading Room of the City of Madison* (July 1, 1879).

> *The first is, to supply the people with rational amusement by an adequate number of entertaining books, which will enable them to agreeably pass the*

> *time, which otherwise would be swallowed up by frivolity, ennui, mental vacuity or something even worse.*

Madison's library moved to its own building in 1906, a Carnegie library on the corner of Carroll and Dayton Streets. A Library School opened on the second floor of the building in the fall of 1906. It remained there for thirty-two years, at which point the school transferred to the University of Wisconsin to give more space to the public library. The Madison Free Library became the Madison Public Library in 1959. It moved to its present site at 201 West Mifflin Street in 1965.[106]

The press, like religion, followed settlement. As settlers move westward, newspapers set up shop on the frontier with astonishing speed. Madison's first printing press arrived with the first legislature in November 1838. It soon produced a four-page weekly called the *Wiskonsin Enquirer* filled with literary works, moralistic editorials, news stories, legal notices and advertising. Madison got a second paper in 1839: the *Wisconsin Express*. Pioneer papers took a hard partisan line, and the editors engaged in sometimes-vicious editorial battles.[107]

Besides politics, many newspapers took a hard line on immigration, commonly treating new arrivals with disdain. Germans and Irish were suspected of "popery" for their Catholic faith. When several Norwegians moved out of Madison, the *Wisconsin State Journal* remarked that the county had lost nothing but a few sheep and cattle by their departure. The *State Journal* also endorsed a method to fool the Irish from participating in the November 1854 election.

The foreign press blossomed in response to this harsh treatment. In the 1850s, German and Norwegian papers like the *Wisconsin Staats-Zeitung*, the *Madison Demokrat* and the *Norsternen* hit Madison streets, its pages filled with ways to participate in politics and fight anti-immigrant sentiment.[108]

Madison's press began to change in the early twentieth century. Previously, the primary reason for owning a newspaper had been to advance a political agenda. But beginning in the late nineteenth century, many editors began to expand their vision of what a newspaper could be, using their pens to advance reform rather than unquestioningly following partisan politics. For the first time, local and reform-oriented news made the front page.

Within the first decades of the twentieth century, two Madison newspapers came to dominate daily news: the *Wisconsin State Journal* and the upstart *The*

Capital Times. It also saw the demise of the *Madison Democrat*, a city institution for fifty-three years that went under after a long battle with the *Wisconsin State Journal* for the hearts of subscribers.

The arrival of Richard Lloyd Jones to the helm of the *Wisconsin State Journal* in 1911 brought big city–style journalism to Madison. Jones hired a large staff to investigate local news and reform issues. He changed the format of the newspaper, introducing a thick Sunday edition of the paper that included a magazine, sports section and color comics.[109] The paper became a powerful voice for the Progressive movement, and Jones himself took bold editorial stances in his own writings. Jones pushed Robert La Follette's agenda forward, advocating for labor reform, women's suffrage and academic freedom while condemning government corruption. Madison residents clearly loved the lively writing and forceful editorials, as circulation surged during Jones's tenure.

World War I challenged Jones's unabashed support of Senator Robert La Follette, however. While many Americans supported American involvement in the war, La Follette strenuously did not. Jones not only strongly disagreed with La Follette but questioned his integrity as well, a position that deeply angered Jones's managing editor, William T. Evjue. As a result, Evjue resigned from the *State Journal* in September 1917 and, three months later, on December 13, 1917, printed the first issue of his own newspaper, *The Capital Times*.[110]

Although it was not the best time to start a newspaper, Evjue persevered, fighting detractors and wartime hysteria that labeled him pro-German for supporting La Follette. Three months after its first issue, *The Capital Times* had fifty-two hundred subscribers—more than the *Madison Democrat* had accumulated in more than fifty years—becoming Madison's second-largest newspaper.[111]

Two years after the war, in February 1921, the *Madison Democrat* announced it was going out of business. The high costs of labor and paper had severely squeezed the newspaper's finances, forcing its editors to raise prices and reduce its size. The *Democrat* was also far less profitable for the Democrat Printing Company than its other publishing ventures. With the loss of the *Democrat*, Madison became a two-paper town, a situation that continued until April 2008, when *The Capital Times* ceased daily publication.

10

INDUSTRY AND ENTREPRENEURIAL SPIRIT

The Farwell boom of the 1850s had given Madison residents confidence in the city's future—a future that many felt certain could only be secured by creating an industrial base for the city. But huge debt from the spending sprees of 1856–57 and the economic recession following the Civil War made it difficult to get Madison's economy moving in any sustained way in the 1870s and 1880s.

Many Madison leaders turned to manufacturing as the most effective and desirable way to grow the economy and the city. They had seen it happen in other cities and had become convinced that it was Madison's best hope. Manufacturing had played a minor role in Madison's economy to date, however, taking a backseat to securing railroads, keeping the capital in town, building city services and promoting the university. At the close of the Civil War, Madison had a flour mill, a woolen factory, a steam planing mill, an iron foundry and little else. The 1866 city directory put it kindly when it said that Madison's manufacturing interests were "not very extensive."[112]

No longer content with buying products from other places, Mayor David Atwood, in his 1868 inaugural address, declared that only factories could "plant a city upon a solid and enduring basis."[113] The *Wisconsin State Journal* and the *Madison Democrat* newspapers quickly followed suit, loudly beating the drum for manufacturing as the key to Madison's future.

Despite the loud support of the mayor and newspapers, community support remained weak. Many complained that Madison did not have enough coal or water power to become a manufacturing center. Factory proponents did not disagree that both were challenges to overcome but countered that the city's water power had never been fully employed. They also pointed to other Wisconsin cities, including Green Bay, Fond du Lac and La Crosse, that had become manufacturing cities without water power. Moreover, they insisted that the price of railroad-delivered coal had fallen far enough to be nearly competitive for manufacturing.[114]

Even if coal did not become affordable, many factory advocates believed they might have found a viable alternative to coal: peat. Composed of partially decayed vegetation, peat is a black spongy material found in wetlands and lakes. Cut into blocks and dried, it produces a hot flame, like coal. Large peat beds discovered in the Madison area after the Civil War could potentially produce steam power for one-third the cost of wood or coal.[115] Spotting an opportunity, Madison businessmen moved to exploit these new resources and formed two peat processing and distribution companies.

Surveying the economic scene for the most likely areas of growth, Madison's factory proponents decided that agricultural implements seemed like the city's best hope. It certainly didn't hurt that the industry had already become Madison's largest single business post Civil War.[116] Most of the implements were simply sold and distributed in Madison, not manufactured here. As more of Dane County's fertile soil came under cultivation, the market for a homegrown implement industry seemed especially promising.

The potential of agricultural implements was not just hype. Madison already had two implement makers, the E.W. Skinner Company and Madison Plow Works, that many expected would form the nucleus of the city's agricultural supply industry.[117] Eager to pick up the pace of the implement business, a group of Madison investors decided to start their own factory in hopes of building the city into a regional manufacturer. The Madison Manufacturing Company opened its doors in 1870. One year later, in 1871, J.H. Garnhart agreed to locate his Garnhart Reaper Works in Madison in exchange for rich financial incentives from the city.[118]

Unfortunately, the nascent agricultural implement industry was hit hard by the 1873 depression that swept the country. The Garnhart Reaper Works, the richly incentivized hope of the agricultural industry, closed.[119] Madison's three other factories managed to stay afloat, but the writing on the wall was clear: Madison's industrial future was not—at least in the immediate future—to be.

But where agricultural implements failed to take hold, the resort industry proved an unexpected success. In 1866, developers George Delaplaine and Elisha Burdick opened the doors of Lakeside House, a sixty-room, four-story resort hotel in the center of what is today Olin Park. This wasn't the building's first time as a hotel. It had originally opened as the Water Cure in 1854 during the Farwell boom as a combination hotel and spa offering all kinds of hydrotherapy. The Water Cure never managed to become a financial success and closed in 1857. Although no resort had ever succeeded in Madison, Delaplaine and Burdick were confident that this time, their resort would not fail.

Conditions were different in Madison than they had been during the Farwell years. Madison now had direct rail access from Chicago, making it easier than ever for tourists to reach by rail. Southerners also began fleeing north in the summer to escape the heat and diseases endemic to southern cities, including cholera and yellow fever.

As its developers predicted, Lakeside House quickly became Madison's first successful resort hotel. With its thirty wooded acres, Lakeside House offered guests panoramic views of the city and surrounding countryside, a concert and promenade hall, hot and cold running water, bathtubs and accessibility to the city by steamboat or road.[120]

Other hotels soon opened to meet growing demand. The first five years of the resort boom saw the opening of Vilas House and Rasdall House. The fancy Park Hotel opened on the Capitol Square in 1871 to provide luxury accommodations to wealthy tourists. It also appeased legislators, who complained that Madison hotels were terrible and had tried to use this as yet another reason to have the capital moved from Madison.

Madison's appeal as a summer destination was sung far and wide in the press. The *Chicago Times*, the *New Orleans Republic*, the *St. Louis Dispatch* and the *Nashville American* were among the newspapers that praised Madison's attractions. Among the notable guests to visit Madison were St. Louis brewers Adolphus Busch and Everhard Anheuser, Civil War general William T. Sherman and President Lincoln's son, Robert T. Lincoln.[121]

The success of the resort industry came at just the right time to get the economy moving. Although some continued to argue that manufacturing was a more stable industry, most residents were happy to let tourism be the engine of growth for the time being.[122]

Another surprise industry was ice harvesting. People had harvested and stored ice—a natural resource that cold Wisconsin winters produced

The remodeled and enlarged Lakeside House opened as a successful resort in 1866 but was destroyed by fire in 1877. *Wisconsin Historical Society Image ID #25114.*

in abundance—in Madison for many years. As iceboxes became more common appliances in homes in the 1860s, city directories listed several men employed in cutting, storing and distributing ice to residents. Unsurprisingly, Madison's five breweries were the biggest consumers of ice, using hundreds of tons of ice to chill their beer.[123]

Madison began exporting ice in 1875. The growing brewing and meatpacking industries in Chicago and Milwaukee needed tremendous quantities of ice, which local sources could not supply alone. Madison's direct rail line to both cities made its ice a natural choice. Americans also loved cold drinks and needed a steady supply of ice to keep their beverages frosty.[124]

The ice trade had grown so large by 1880 that Madison residents began to speak of an "ice boom." So many men worked in the industry that 150 boxcars filled with ice left the city daily.[125] The ice industry was, in many ways, a perfect industry for Madison because it employed hundreds of men during the winter season, when so many were unemployed, and it only grew during the depression of the 1870s, when other industries downsized. Ice remained a major Madison business for thirty years.

By the late nineteenth century, business and civic leaders were desperate to find something that would make Madison boom, an industry that would attract people, money and jobs. The resort industry had enjoyed a nice boom for a while, but the depression of the 1870s and the seasonal nature of the work had led to its decline by 1880. Madison's stagnating population particularly embarrassed city leaders, as Madison fell from Wisconsin's second most populous city in the 1850s to its sixth by the 1880 census.

Not everyone was unhappy with Madison's weak manufacturing sector, however. Quite a few leaders liked Madison's role as the center of education and government rather than smokestacks. They favored growth and change only if it enhanced the city's reputation as the intellectual leader of the state.[126]

Fortunately, manufacturing interests began to come together in a more promising way. In January 1880, Norwegian immigrant John A. Johnson and Yankee businessman Morris E. Fuller joined forces and purchased the Madison Plow Company. A few months later, they bought a vacant factory at the corner of Dickinson and East Washington and began manufacturing plows and cultivators.[127] They changed the name of the company to Fuller and Johnson Manufacturing Company and became, in only three short years, Madison's most successful commercial enterprise.[128]

Fuller and Johnson took advantage of the growing market for farm machinery as settlers poured onto the plains and prairies of the Dakotas, Kansas, Nebraska and Colorado in the 1880s.[129] The company built its fortune on the Bonanza Prairie Breaker, a sod-breaking plow ideal for the prairie terrain faced by homesteaders. It also manufactured horse-drawn plows, cultivators, harrows and mowers. By 1899, Fuller and Johnson had sales topping $1 million annually. More importantly for Madison, the company gave the city the industrial respectability it craved.[130]

Even as Johnson was building his implement company, he had begun to think about starting another factory: one that manufactured machine tools. Machine tools manufacture parts for other machines. At the time, Johnson and Fuller purchased machine tools from other places to make its implements—why not make tools for its own machines and to sell to others?

In January 1889, Johnson incorporated his new enterprise and called it Gisholt Machine Company, named for his aunt's farm in Norway. Johnson hired his three sons to construct the factory, and by 1890, a handful of workers had moved in. The company became known for its turret lathes, a heavy-duty machine capable of grinding eighteen- to twenty-four-inch castings that was not available from anyone else at the time. Gisholt lathes won a gold medal at the 1900 World's Fair in Paris against the best machine tool manufacturers in the world, virtually ensuring Johnson a flourishing business.

Johnson's companies left a lasting mark on Madison. The location of his factories on the marsh east of the capitol encouraged other factories to move into the area, creating a factory district on the east side of town.[131] This geographic district became cemented in Madison with a turn-of-the-twentieth-century agreement to keep factories on the east side of town and homes to the west, creating the east-west divide that continues to this day. Johnson's factories also attracted a highly skilled labor force that earned some of the highest wages in Wisconsin.[132] Moreover, Johnson helped to convince those citizens opposed to industrial growth that factories were not necessarily detrimental to the city and could provide positive benefit.

Although Johnson's factories were the largest in the late nineteenth century, they were not the only factories to take hold in Madison. Smaller companies sprang up that produced everything from corsets and cigars to bicycles, beer, telephones and underwear.[133] Dane County's leading crop, tobacco, had only a minor effect on Madison. Several tobacco-sorting warehouses opened, but most of the processing business went to smaller communities located near the tobacco growing fields.[134]

The United States Sugar Factory opened the largest factory building in the area in the village of Fair Oaks, to the east of Madison, in 1906. Making sugar from sugar beets, the factory encouraged farmers to grow beets by offering high prices and providing well-paying jobs. At its peak, the factory ran twenty-four hours a day, seven days a week, producing fifty tons of sugar a day. Cheap foreign imports caused United States Sugar to go bankrupt in 1924.[135]

Manufacturing was not the only growth area in Madison. City merchants, too, began to experience economic expansion. Between 1880 and 1885, the number of businesses on the Capitol Square grew from 89 to 124. Furniture, hardware, books, clothing, jewelry, baked goods and shoes were among the goods that could be purchased on the square in 1885. The streets were also home to ten saloons.[136]

According to the *Wisconsin State Journal*, the growth in business downtown resulted from merchants displaying their goods more attractively and offering more selection, all of which drew more shoppers than ever before. Merchants also supported city efforts to promote Madison to tourists, state fair goers and conventioneers because all would increase their business. Implement dealers and distributors set up showrooms to market agricultural machines. Some manufacturers built their own factory outlet stores, while others rented space in Implement Row, an L-shaped district that offered everything a farmer could ever want.[137]

Together, these merchants and manufacturers contributed to the entrepreneurial spirit that characterized the late nineteenth century in Madison, helping to propel the city forward into a new century.

11
PROGRESSIVE POLITICS

As the nineteenth century drew to a close, many observers could see that the transformation of frontier Madison into a bustling capital city had caused problems no one had anticipated in 1836. Madison's growth had created more jobs and more opportunities but also more poverty, disease and crime. Many citizens were trapped at the bottom rungs of the city. The democratic institutions crafted for the city and state had evolved into a closed system that mainly benefited wealthy residents and party insiders. Something had to change.

The "endless numbers of things to be done"[138] frustrated some Madison leaders in 1900. But this frustration had its constructive side, according to historian David Mollenhoff. Many felt a growing resolve to make Madison a much better city, the city they all felt Madison had the potential of becoming. This transformation would require work, though, and would come by pairing human energy with powerful organizations to lead the city in a new direction.[139]

One of those new organizations, the Progressives, believed it had a plan that would bring results. Progressivism was a national movement of people concerned about the deteriorating conditions of the nation's cities, the growing concentration of wealth and the increasing oppression of workers. Locally, Progressives presented a vision of Madison with an efficient and more powerful local government, free of partisanship and more responsive to the needs of everyday people; a city with clean lakes and beautiful parks, free of slums and poverty. Although this was a national movement, no state became more associated with progressivism than Wisconsin and no man more so than Madison's own Robert La Follette.

The genesis of La Follette's progressivism reputedly occurred on September 17, 1891, when Republican Philetus Sawyer offered the thirty-five-year-old attorney a bribe to fix a court case. Furious that Sawyer would try to use money to influence the legal system, La Follette refused and angrily denounced the use of money to shut out the voice of the people. For the rest of the decade, he traveled around Wisconsin, speaking out against crooked politicians, powerful lumber barons and corrupt railroad interests. Elected governor in 1900, La Follette pledged to institute reforms to make government responsive to the people rather than business.

During his three terms as governor, La Follette successfully pushed the legislature to pass measures instituting direct primary elections, giving voters the right to choose their own candidates for office. He convinced the legislature to pass railroad regulation, broke up business monopolies, preserved state forests, protected workers' rights, defended small farmers and worked to reduce the influence of special interests. La Follette's techniques and ideas made him and Wisconsin national symbols of Progressive experimentation.

One of his experiments was the "laboratory of democracy," the enlistment of specialists in law, economics and the social and natural sciences from the University of Wisconsin to draft laws, offer advice and serve on government commissions.

"The Wisconsin Idea," as it came to be called, held that an effective and accountable government worked best with the help of experts in the area in question. University of Wisconsin professors John R. Commons and Edwin Witte worked closely with Progressive politicians to create programs that benefited workers, consumers and the disadvantaged. A new Legislative Reference Bureau headed by Charles McCarthy provided lawmakers with the services of trained researchers and a bill-drafting office that was emulated around the world.

When La Follette resigned as governor after his election to the Senate in 1906, many feared that the university-government connection would disappear. Instead, the connection endured and played a major role in the development of several key pieces of legislation, including the Civil Service Law, workers compensation and the implementation of the initiative and referendum.

The desire for reform in cities across the country produced countless single-purpose organizations dedicated to specific problems and reforms. In Madison, reform came through alternate means: the state legislature. Experience had taught many Madison reformers that organizations and exhortations to change had only a minimal effect. Enduring change could only happen through governmental action. Although most of the Progressive legislation focused on state programs, many had direct applications to local government.

Municipal reform in Madison began in the mayor's office. The city's weak mayor and strong city council system had left the mayor with too little power to be effective. The aldermen held all the real power; they developed the city budget, approved expenditures, passed local legislation and created city policies. To increase the mayor's power, the legislature first extended the term from one to two years. This extra year would allow the mayor more time to get to know the government and hopefully be more effective as a result.

Soon after the term extension went into effect, reformers pushed to give the mayor a salary. Proponents argued that good executive talent did not come free, especially as the city grew and the job became more complex and time consuming. Madison began paying its mayors $1,000 a year in 1908, far less than reformers wanted but all that the city council would approve.[140]

Among Madison's more radical reformers, an extended term and salary did not go far enough: they wanted to change the office itself. What they proposed was a commission government, rule by a group of officials rather than a single person, a system that had worked with extraordinary effect in reviving Galveston, Texas, after a hurricane devastated the city in 1900.[141] Despite support from some of Madison's leading citizens and the *Wisconsin State Journal*, however, a referendum on abolishing the mayor-council system in favor of a commission government failed.[142]

While commission backers did not give up, the Wisconsin legislature soon passed an impressive array of bills that helped to remedy many of the problems of the weak mayor/strong council government. One such bill was the 1911 Corrupt Practices Act, which outlawed the custom of plying voters with beer and other gifts on behalf of particular parties and candidates.[143] Along with the 1911 Referendum Act, the 1903 Direct Primary Act, the 1911 Initiative Act and the 1913 Recall Act helped make local government more responsive to citizens.

Another highly influential bill was the 1912 Non-Partisan Act, which eliminated partisanship from local elections.[144] Candidates would now run on the basis of their merits rather than as members of a political party. The law was first applied to Madison's aldermanic elections in 1913 and to the mayoral election in 1914. The act also encouraged politicians to develop platforms rather than rely solely on emotional partisan appeals. Party endorsements and personal testimonials would no longer satisfy voters who wanted candidates to have ideas for bringing about change.[145]

Far less glamorous but an enduring mark of good governance was the reformation of the city budgeting system. From the time Madison became a city, aldermen had spent money freely, with little supervision or forethought. No one kept track of who was spending what and for what, and many funds were gone long before the year was up, a practice that often left the city levying a catch-up tax to pay for the previous year's reckless spending.[146] The adoption of a new system that required budgets to be prepared in advance with all monies received and expended accounted for was far more time-consuming but allowed Madison to have, for the first time, a clear picture of its financial status.[147]

Madison also got a new capitol building. Early in the morning on February 27, 1904, night watchman Nat Cramton smelled smoke and ran to the assembly cloakroom, where he found the ceiling ablaze. The Madison Fire Department was called, but when it arrived, no water would come from the capitol hydrants. By the time the firemen managed to hook their hoses to the city water mains, the fire had spread to most of the south wing. Governor La Follette, awakened with the news of the fire about 4:00 a.m., rushed into the burning building, where for three hours he helped evacuate government records and other valuables. When the fire was finally extinguished, the east, west and south wings lay in ruins, nearly 80 percent of the building.

Although the fire was unexpected, it wasn't a complete disaster. Plans for a new, bigger capitol were already underway when the flames consumed the current structure. The commission held a competition to find the best design for the new capitol. Of the five entrants, the New York firm of George B. Post and Sons won the committee's unanimous support. Construction began in late 1907 and was finally finished in 1917.[148]

In addition to making structural, financial and administrative changes, Madison Progressives sought to improve the city's moral climate as well. Although never as raucously vice-ridden as other western towns, Madison

A devastating fire destroyed Madison's second capitol building on February 26–27, 1904. *Wisconsin Historical Society Image ID #1906.*

had its share of unsavory characters, drinking, prostitution and gambling. The focal point of much of this moral crusade focused, as it long had, on the saloon.

The saloon was Madison's most popular and most reviled institution. Many of Madison's early settlers had come from New England, which was a stronghold of the temperance-advocating "drys." Madison had levied a heavy fine on anyone who sold liquor in 1846, but the law was overturned a year later by a three-to-one majority of pro-saloon "wets." Crusades against the saloon continued throughout the nineteenth century, as temperance advocates and prohibitionists signed abstinence pledges, joined organizations like the Woman's Christian Temperance Union and held prayer vigils for saloon patrons. To these dry advocates, the elimination of the saloon was the only answer.

Temperance represented something far more complicated than a simple battle between those who drank and those who did not in Madison. German

Madison's current capitol building, its third, was finished in 1917. *Erika Janik.*

immigrants, mostly Catholic, often remained strongly attached to their historical and cultural roots, an attachment that included saloons and drinking on Sundays, both generally abhorrent to Yankees. These immigrants also frequently took uniform stands on political and social issues and resisted efforts to assimilate to Yankee cultural norms, which included Protestantism and quiet observance of the Sabbath day. Temperance, therefore, became symbolic of battles between Yankees and Germans, between teetotaling Protestants and broad-minded Catholics.

Although devoted to their cause, temperance campaigns produced more ridicule than actual results. In the 1890s, two referenda on the wet/dry issue produced comfortable margins of victory for the wets. Prohibitionists even had trouble getting officials to enforce the law requiring saloons to be closed on Sundays.[149] Faced with this discouraging situation, and with the number of saloons growing faster than the population, temperance leaders decided to change course. They moved away from prohibition and the total elimination of the saloon in favor of making it more difficult and more expensive to drink.[150]

Armed with their new goal, Madison drys attempted to make it too expensive for saloons to operate by passing a referendum raising the price of liquor licenses from $200 to $500 in 1901. Voters turned down the high fee, which would have closed about 20 percent of the city's saloons, but the nine percentage points separating them from victory nevertheless encouraged the drys to keep fighting.[151]

Three years later, in August 1904, the city created a twenty-two-block, saloon-free zone surrounding the Fuller and Johnson and Gisholt factories on East Washington Avenue to discourage drinking among workers. A similar zone had been established in 1897 around the University of Wisconsin. The university zone was expanded in 1907 to within a half-mile radius of Bascom Hall, a distance that stopped just short of the Hausmann Brewery on State and Gorham Streets.[152]

With rising anti-saloon sentiment, temperance leaders introduced another referendum to raise the liquor license fee in September 1907. Saloonkeepers launched a counteroffensive, threatening to stop serving the popular free lunch and to serve beer in smaller glasses if the fee was raised. Despite these efforts, the referendum passed, and the cost to operate a saloon rose to $500.[153]

Buoyed by their win, Madison drys began to think that maybe a total prohibition was possible. In 1912, they formed the Madison Prohibition

Party and fielded a mayoral candidate. Their candidate took nearly a quarter of the votes but cut into the tally of the dry Republican candidate, giving the election to the wet Democrat John B. Heim. Although they lost the election, the Prohibitionist Party platform was decidedly Progressive, calling for public ownership of utilities, a civil service and a commission form of government, all reforms the saloon lobby opposed. But by aligning themselves on the side of reform, the prohibitionists were becoming fast friends with Madison's Progressives, a smart place to be in the early twentieth century.[154]

Over the next few years, several developments helped propel the prohibitionists forward in their quest. Enrollment at the University of Wisconsin grew rapidly after the establishment of the saloon-free, half-mile zone around the campus as parents felt it was once again safe to send their children to Madison. Madison got its own affiliate of the national Anti-Saloon League, an organization recognized for its effective dry campaigns, known as the Madison Dry League. The Dry League, soon five hundred members strong, helped defeat Heim in his 1914 reelection campaign, a stunning defeat for an incumbent, and helped elect dry Republican Adolph Kayser.

Prohibitionists were gaining strength not just in Madison but also around the country. An astonishing 87 percent of U.S. counties had voted themselves dry by 1916, though most large cities stayed wet.[155] The 1916 election brought a large dry contingent to the Wisconsin State Assembly, including *Wisconsin State Journal* business manager and part-time reporter William T. Evjue. Soon after he was elected, Evjue introduced a statewide wet/dry referendum that passed both houses but was vetoed by Governor Emanuel Philipp on the grounds that it would cost thousands of brewery workers their jobs.[156] To curb the growth of saloons, the legislature passed a law limiting the number of saloons to no more than one for every five hundred persons, an act that forced Madison's city council to cut the number of saloons to just sixty-four, the fewest since 1888.[157]

The coming of World War I gave the drys another peg to hang prohibition on: patriotism. With grain and coal in high demand for the Allied war effort, using these supplies to make alcohol seemed increasingly unnecessary and wasteful, not to mention anti-American. The strategy worked, and on April 3, 1917, Madison residents voted themselves dry. Nearly a year and a half before national Prohibition, the city's remaining saloons closed their doors on June 30, 1917. The Breckheimer Brewery closed as well, but significantly, the Fauerbach and Hasmann Breweries kept right on brewing. The law only prevented them from selling beer in Madison, not from selling beer altogether. So they set up warehouses in Middleton to sell their beer to thirsty residents, even providing a delivery service for those who could not make the trek.[158]

Nationally, Prohibition moved ever close to reality. The Anti-Saloon League had helped to elect enough supporters to Congress that, in December 1918, Congress approved the Eighteenth Amendment banning the manufacture and sale of intoxicating beverages. One year later, on January 16, 1919, the final state ratified the amendment. The nation went dry one year later on January 16, 1920.

Drinking was not the only issue to raise the ire of Madison's moral crusaders in the early twentieth century, however. Prostitution and gambling were two other social ills, tightly linked to saloons but also separate problems. Many saloons had slot machines up front and back rooms where prostitutes could ply their trade. Although gambling machines were illegal, police only casually enforced the law, and the common council routinely issued licenses to saloons boasting both back rooms and gambling machines.[159]

Prostitution did not just occur in the saloons, though. Madison was also home to several whorehouses that operated openly. The city's most famous was the Blue Goose, located in the middle of the marsh to the east of downtown at 911 East Mifflin Street. The area, surrounded by marshy plants and little-used roads, was an ideal location for patrons to come and go in relative obscurity. The women of the Blue Goose came from Chicago and catered to respectable men, both young and old.[160]

Police raids of these houses proved unsuccessful in providing permanent results. A raid in one house simply led to a new house opening in another part of town. Some madams did open houses outside of town to lessen the hassles of dealing with the city.[161]

The crackdown on gambling and prostitution did begin to pay off eventually. In 1903, the common council outlawed back rooms in saloons. The next year, in 1904, the newly elected mayor, Dexter Curtis, launched an attack on prostitution and gambling; it was so successful that both vices were nearly eliminated from the city. Stories of prostitution arrests virtually disappeared from the newspaper after 1906.[162]

One issue on which Madison and the rest of Wisconsin were not so progressive was the rights of women. Women's rights had first come to the fore in Wisconsin in the 1840s at the urging of some utopian dreamers who believed that women's rights should be legally protected. During the 1850s, a flood of new immigrants, political corruption and an economic crash dampened much of the utopian energy in Wisconsin, while the Civil War largely dislodged it from the popular mind for an entire generation. For the next half century, women remained consigned to the home, charged with raising children, preparing food, making clothes and cleaning.

Groups focusing on suffrage (and often temperance, too) became more common in the late 1860s. The largest group to organize, the Wisconsin Women's Suffrage Association (WWSA), formed in 1869 to begin a statewide campaign. Because many suffrage activists were also leaders in the state's temperance movement, the movement generated additional hostility from the state's powerful brewing industry and from German Americans. They feared that if given the opportunity, women would vote overwhelmingly for prohibition, a compelling reason to keep women out of the voting booths.

The heavy involvement of women in the drive to improve public schools, a trend that seemed acceptable to many male policymakers, gave them some success with suffrage. In 1869, the state legislature passed a law allowing women to run for school boards and other elective school offices. Neighboring states began allowing women to vote in elections related to school and temperance issues in the 1870s. Following their success in gaining the right to run for local school boards, the WWSA began an all-out suffrage campaign in the legislature in 1884. The legislature refused to consider full suffrage but gave women the right to vote in any election with school issues on the ballot in 1885. This law, along with the creation of women's clubs and the increase in the number of women attending college, led to an intensified discussion on the role of women as the nineteenth century drew to a close.

Although home to a number of men with more liberal views on women, Madison remained a highly sexist society in the early twentieth century. The school had separate playgrounds for boys and girls. Private schools offered education to boys or girls, but not to both in one place. And at the Vilas Hotel, men could sit on the veranda while women were relegated to the balcony only.[163]

Everything would begin to change over the next two decades, though, as a growing number of women began to demand a more equal place in the world.

Women's clubs were the locus of the first expansion of women's roles into civic affairs, a role seen as congruent with their domestic responsibilities. Dr. Samuel E. Sparling, a UW political scientist and Fifth Ward alderman, was one of the first to publicly broach the idea of an expanded role for women in city problems. In a speech in 1900 to the Woman's Club entitled "How May Women Assist in the Government of Our Cities?" Sparling claimed that many of the problems facing the city—crowded schools, dirty lakes and streets and poor garbage collection—were actually "home questions," women's traditional domain. As such, many of these issues actually belonged to women, who thus had an obligation to "develop a wholesome physical and moral environment in the city."[164]

With this expanded field of play and organizations such as the Woman's Club, founded in 1893, the Civics Club (1913), the Catholic Women's Club (1914) and the Girls Civic League, women began working on problems in education, health, housing, morals, recreation and charity.[165] City leaders in both parties supported the idea. Liberals loved the idea of giving women an expanded role in municipal affairs, while conservatives liked that it did not seem to threaten traditional male roles by hewing to the idea of home and women's domestic responsibilities. The success of these organizations in implementing reforms led to tremendous growth in membership as more women than ever before saw a chance to take on a larger public role.

More women began working outside the home, too. Stores, offices and factories offered women a growing number of jobs. By 1920, more than 32 percent of Madison women over the age of sixteen worked outside the home.[166] Because the job market was tightly controlled by men, most women worked long hours at low-paying and low-skill jobs. Seamstresses, laundresses, store clerks, typists and maids were among the most common occupations. Even when men and women worked the same jobs, such as schoolteachers, women still earned less than men.[167]

Women still remained far behind at the polls. After many decades of agitation but little real progress, the suffrage movement changed tenor in the 1890s. While the first wave of the suffrage movement had advocated radical rather than gradual change, a new generation of suffrage activists began to work for more incremental reforms. Led by Theodora Winton Youmans of Waukesha and Ada James of Richland Center, women's rights advocates began relying heavily on women's clubs to promote suffrage as just one part of a broader platform of civic reform. The WWSA gave way to the Wisconsin Federation of Women's Clubs (WFWC) as the leader in the campaign for women's rights.

These new reformers concentrated on two short-term goals: placing more women in influential state government positions and making the school suffrage law actually work. In 1901, the legislature finally authorized separate school ballots, enabling women to vote for school offices. La Follette, whose wife, Belle, was an attorney active in the women's movement, advanced the first goal by appointing women to state boards and commissions. He also helped pass laws that ensured that women would always have positions on some state boards.

But the same Progressive leaders who endorsed worker and consumer rights were reluctant to grant women suffrage because they knew their male supporters opposed it. On November 4, 1912, Wisconsin men voted suffrage down two to one.

When politicians blocked new suffrage referenda in 1913 and 1915, Wisconsin women threw their energy behind a national voting campaign. A suffrage amendment to the U.S. Constitution finally passed in 1919, and as if to compensate for years of intractable opposition, the Wisconsin legislature became the first to ratify it on June 10, 1919, giving women the right to vote in federal elections. The right to vote in state elections did not come until 1934, however, when the Wisconsin constitution was finally amended. Wisconsin did pass the nation's first equal rights bill in 1921, granting women full equality with men under civil law. Unfortunately, the generalities of the law and its subjection to court interpretation rendered the law essentially meaningless for women.

To many Madison residents, the early twentieth century offered a host of targets for reform, many of which the Progressives attacked with impressive results. The Progressives greatly expanded the power of local government in response to public demands for more and better services. They turned to experts for advice on issues and problems facing the city. They also created a heightened sense of community by focusing on issues that they believed aided civic virtue and civic welfare. Although in some ways incomplete, spotty and occurring in fits and starts, the Progressive movement was notable for the dedication of politicians and citizens to improvement, expansion, growth and change and for Progressives' firm belief in their ability to make the world a better place for everyone.

12
PLANNING FOR THE FUTURE

Of all the cities in the United States, it appears to me that Madison has the best opportunity" to become "a model American city," proclaimed John Nolen in his 1911 plan for the city. "With a form and flavor unlike that of any other place," Nolen confidently asserted that Madison had all the necessary features to "establish a new standard for city making in the United States."[168]

When the City of Madison hired the walrus-mustached John Nolen in 1908, it had little idea what it was getting. But the plan that he produced for the city in 1911 presented an audacious and far-reaching vision of what Madison could become with the right leadership and goals. Never before (and never since) had a city plan captured the sense of Madison's destiny so clearly and so eloquently. Nolen's vision, even if only incrementally realized in the succeeding years, has inspired and challenged city leaders and residents for generations.

Nolen came to Madison at a time when few people had ever heard of city planning. At the same time, however, some prominent leaders and citizens in the late nineteenth century had begun to be troubled by the ugly shapelessness and poverty of American cities. Many cities had simply developed too quickly to concern themselves with the quality and beauty of that growth, not to mention its adverse impact on residents. Beauty, along with moral and municipal reforms, came to drive efforts to improve American cities around the turn of the twentieth century as part of what came to be called the City Beautiful movement.

Landscape architect John Nolen, who devised a plan for the future growth and development of Madison. *Wisconsin Historical Society Image ID #12506.*

"Not only have we been negligent to improve our appearance and convenience, but we have about destroyed the original beauty and the approaches to our lake borders by allowing encroachments—nuisances—as unsightly as unlawful," wrote an angry Napolean Bonaparte Van Slyke, president of Madison's First National Bank, in a letter to the *Wisconsin State Journal* in January 1893. Van Slyke was certainly not alone in this sentiment. Doty's original plat of Madison had included only one public space, a park around the capitol building, and completely ignored the opportunities presented by the lakes. Civic leaders urged the elimination of unsightly buildings and the cleaning of city streets. In the words of historian David Mollenhoff, never before had so many leaders been so strongly in favor of flowers, fountains, boulevards and trees.[169]

To carry out these beautification plans, the Madison Improvement Association organized in 1893. Public support for the association was high: within two weeks of forming, the association had received $11,000 in pledges for its projects.[170]

The Madison Improvement Association focused its early efforts in three areas: tree planting, park development and street and lakeshore beautification. To facilitate tree planting, the association sold low-cost trees to homeowners and instructed them on how to care and maintain them. They hired Chicago landscape architect Olaf Benson to design parks, boulevards and walkways for the city. They also hired Frank Lloyd Wright, a former Madison resident but now a rising Chicago architect, to design two public boathouses, one on Lake Mendota and the other on Lake Monona.[171] Unfortunately, community opposition coupled with the severe 1893 depression kept many of these projects from ever being realized.

The depression did not spell the end of beautification in Madison, however. Just as the Madison Improvement Association organized, another group of men was collaborating to create Madison's first pleasure drive, a project that profoundly influenced the city's beautification movement.

Horse-drawn carriage rides through the countryside surrounding Madison were a favorite recreational activity for families and courting couples in the second half of the nineteenth century. Designed for leisurely tours, these drives wound through trees, over hills and along shorelines, earning them the name "pleasure drives." The University of Wisconsin had opened a network of farm roads and pleasure drives to the public in the 1860s through its campus farm. These roads were connected with additional segments at

Eagle Heights and along Owens Road in the early 1890s with the help of lawyer and UW law professor John M. Olin. The new twelve-mile road officially opened in October 1892.[172]

The newly constructed drive proved a great success and soon led to the formation of the Madison Park and Pleasure Drive Association in 1894, with Olin as its leader. The new association aimed to create more roadways in and around Madison that allowed for a scenic escape from the frenetic city life. A second major pleasure drive opened in 1897 around the eastern end of Lake Mendota from Burrows Park to Mendota Mental Health Institute. Not to be outdone, Lake Monona's shoreline residents insisted that they, too, needed a pleasure drive around their lake, a demand that ultimately resulted in the large number of parks and drives that surround much of the lake today.[173]

Although green spaces were becoming increasingly popular, the city did little to support their creation. Responding to the city's inaction, the Madison Park and Pleasure Drive Association decided to expand its reach about 1900, becoming, in effect, Madison's unofficial parks department. The decision came as a result of Daniel Tenney's wish to turn a fourteen-acre parcel along the Yahara River near Lake Mendota into a park. Tenney purchased the land in 1899 and, knowing that the city had a history of refusing to spend money on open spaces, went to Olin with his vision: he would donate the land along with $2,500 to the Madison Park and Pleasure Drive Association as long as the association promised to turn it into a park and to hold it in trust for the city.

Although parks were outside the association's purview, which had, to this point, concerned itself with developing scenic drives outside city limits, the offer was hard to resist. Parks, the association believed, were essential to healthy cities. Olin, along with his association board, knew all too well how few open spaces Madison had; Orton Park, a block of land in the Marquette neighborhood, was the city's only publicly owned space.[174]

Given the city's reluctance to invest in city parks, the association accepted Tenney's offer. Development on the newly named Tenney Park began in 1900. The decision to accept Tenney's gift did not just change the association's mission; it also changed its audience. Instead of bringing mostly wealthy residents to the country, the association would now be bringing the country to the people. To raise funds for the project and to broaden the membership base, Olin slashed the annual membership fee from twenty-five to five dollars and the membership increased tenfold.[175] Money poured in from hardworking families eager for a little breathing space close to home.

Olin then came up with a wildly ambitious plan to deepen and widen the Yahara River, construct a lock, raise all eight bridges and create a twenty-acre parkway linking Lake Monona to Lake Mendota along the river.[176] To make his vision a reality, Olin lobbied the city council and the legislature. He talked landowners into donating their river frontage and convinced the railroads to raise their bridges. Amazingly, Olin got everyone to agree, and the whole project was done in less than three years.

The success of the Yahara Parkway initiated a flood of park philanthropy. In 1904, William Vilas gave the association $18,000 to create a park in honor of his deceased son, Henry, on the shores of Lake Wingra. One year later, in 1905, Thomas E. Brittingham gave $8,000 for a twenty-seven-acre park around Monona Bay, and in 1909, George Burrows donated his fifteen-acre estate on Lake Mendota to the association.[177] Not all of the money came from the wealthy, either. More than seven hundred Madison households contributed to the effort to buy, develop and maintain city parks. About 60 percent of those donations were for five dollars, the minimum membership level in the association.[178]

The number of Madison acres in parkland exploded under the association's guidance. By 1905, city-owned park acreage had increased from 3 acres in 1900 to 154 acres.

Despite all these gains, Olin knew that the long-term sustainability of a park system required city involvement. The city, however, hoped that Olin and the association would continue to build parks for them. Undeterred, Olin worked tirelessly to convince the city to take control, finally scoring two major victories.

In 1905, the common council agreed to hire its first park superintendent to oversee daily park operations. The new position was to be selected and overseen by the association but paid for by the city. This post helped to relieve Olin of an increasingly heavy burden.

Olin's second victory came in 1909, when he convinced the common council to pass a tax of one-half mill, or one twentieth of one cent, for park purposes. He had argued for years that voluntary contributions were uncertain and inadequate to the task of properly caring for the city's parks. In 1902, the city had raised its first bonds for park development, but not without considerable delays and dickering.[179] The tax represented a serious victory for Olin and brought in nearly $50,000 a year for the next decade, more than $28,000 above the voluntary contributions the association managed to collect at its peak. Nearly all of the money collected was turned over to the association, reflecting the city's confidence in its work.[180]

How to use the money ignited debate among association members about the purpose of parks. Some thought that parks should be aesthetic spaces with flowers, trees, rolling meadows and curving pathways, a real escape for working people. Working people often had a different idea, however; they did not just want to look at nature, they wanted to play and be entertained. Taking its cue from residents, the association took down its "keep-off-the-grass signs and learned to tolerate damaged turf," coming to see parks as places where recreation in many forms—picnics, music, swimming and sports—was welcome.[181]

As a result of its work, the Madison Park and Pleasure Drive Association earned national and international renown. City officials from other states came to Madison to inspect the association's work, and many more wrote seeking information and guidance. Association members made presentations, and newspapers around the country touted their work. But to Madison city

James Madison Park on the shores of Lake Mendota is one of the many city green spaces Madison residents now enjoy. *Erika Janik.*

leaders, the real credit for the Madison Park and Pleasure Drive Association belonged to John Olin, its founder, president and tireless advocate.

Not everything Olin proposed came to fruition, though. A few key landowners on Lake Monona stymied his efforts to create a pleasure drive around the lake, despite years of effort. He also failed to create a grand mall connecting the capitol with Lake Monona. Development of Monona Lake Park, now known as B.B. Clarke Beach and Park, took fifteen frustration-filled years.[182]

These failures did not diminish his chief and revolutionary accomplishment: convincing Madison that parks were not frills and that city government had an obligation to provide open spaces to its citizens.

Olin's health forced him to resign as president of the association in 1909, but not before he hired the man who would give Madison a radical new vision of itself: John Nolen.

It all began when Emil Mische, Madison's first park superintendent, asked the city for a $300 raise in 1907. The Madison Park and Pleasure Drive Association urged the city to approve the raise, but the council refused, so Mische took a better-paying job in Portland, Oregon.[183]

Mische's departure gave Olin an opportunity. He had a grand dream for Madison and needed someone with sophisticated skills to help him carry it out. He found that person in John Nolen.

In practice for only two years when Olin hired him, Nolen already had major design contracts in Roanoke, Virginia; Savannah, Georgia; San Diego, California; and Charlotte, North Carolina. A trip to Europe in 1904 had convinced Nolen of the value of an active local government in improving land use and economic development. Despite completing his training in the heyday of the City Beautiful movement, Nolen came to believe that looking good was not enough: cities had to work well, too, integrating plans for housing, transportation, recreation and business.[184]

Olin knew that Nolen was the right man for the job, and he managed to pull together enough money to convince the rising star to come to Madison. In March 1908, the city council gave Nolen a three-year contract to design the city's parks and boulevards.[185]

Olin had more than just parks in mind when he hired Nolen, however. Together, he hoped they could remake Madison, to make it not only beautiful but also clean, humane and economically vibrant. Nolen made a positive impression at his first public presentation at the annual Madison Park and

Pleasure Drive Association meeting in 1908. He praised Madison's beauty and the work done by the association but said that only a city plan would allow Madison to attain its highest potential.[186]

Nolen spent several weeks in Madison studying his new project. Returning to Madison in December 1908, Nolen did not mince words in his assessment of the city. State Street was too narrow and misaligned, railroad crossings were dangerous, the lakeshore was wasted, children had no playgrounds and the city had been careless in planting trees and placing utilities.[187] Haphazard and uncontrolled growth had created these consequences, Nolen told Madison residents. He again stressed that a comprehensive city plan was the way to urban excellence.[188]

Olin needed no convincing. And it did not take him long to convince other city leaders, who joined a Committee of Fifty to oversee the preparation and publication of Nolen's plan.

Nolen submitted his plan to the committee in late August 1910. In designing his plan, Nolen had sought to build on Madison's most unique features: its unrivaled site, its association-shaped public spirit (exemplified by the Madison Park and Pleasure Drive Association) and its role as a center of government, learning and living.

The plan that resulted was both critical and inspirational. The centerpiece of Nolen's plan was the Grand Mall and the Great Esplanade, an elaborate expanse of land and government buildings linking Lake Monona with the capitol. The proposed mall covered twenty acres flanked by classically designed government buildings that cascaded into an esplanade along the lake featuring trees and fountains. He recommended widening State Street and burying city utilities. He called for the beautification of city entrances, the establishment of a strong tree-planting program and the creation of an arboretum at the University of Wisconsin.

Besides beauty, Nolen also suggested ways to make Madison more humane and efficient. His recommendations covered housing, recreation and transportation. He called for low-income housing, playgrounds, more parks, public access to the lakefronts and more controls on railroad development.[189]

Nolen did not gloss over Madison's problems either. He saw foolish planning decisions everywhere he looked. But he also believed that change was possible with the right leadership. Nolen urged Madison residents to think of the "common welfare" as they moved forward, rather than continuing on the path to "community poverty," which had gotten them into their current urban troubles.

John Nolen drew this plan for a park on the corner of Broom and Gorham Streets. *Wisconsin Historical Society Image ID #40669.*

Released to the public in September 1910 and published in March 1911 as *Madison: A Model City*, Nolen's plan arrived with a thud. The exuberance that greeted the idea of a visionary plan for Madison in early 1909 had virtually disappeared a year and a half later. The *Wisconsin State Journal* and the *Madison Democrat* noted its release, but with little fanfare. Rarely had something so potentially revolutionary to the future of the city been dropped so quickly. What happened?

Part of the problem was Olin's retirement. Strong interest and support for city planning remained confined to a small group of leaders led by Olin. After Olin retired in 1909, aldermen who opposed spending city money on parks saw their chance. In February 1910, several aldermen tried to delete Nolen's salary from the budget, even before he had finished a first draft. They failed in this first attempt but came back one year later and successfully cut his salary, effectively firing Nolen before his plan was even published.[190]

Some of this anti-planning sentiment may have come from Nolen's critical views of the city. Although Nolen expressed his criticism professionally, he was still telling city leaders and residents that they had not effectively cared for people and place. Many residents simply rejected his message, defensively choosing instead to see Madison as the state's most beautiful and forward-looking city.

The adoption of Nolen's plan would also have required the government to take on significant new powers and to spend a huge amount of money, nearly all of which Madison leaders had proven reluctant to support. "Large and permanent results are possible only through the regular machinery of city government," wrote Nolen. He also called on citizens to contribute "their share toward the expenses that are necessarily involved." Residents would not only need to accept new rules on land use but also pay for the implementation and maintenance of city programs.[191]

No fool, Nolen recognized that there was no way a city the size of Madison could afford his plan. He was also familiar with the city's previous reluctance to invest in beautification efforts. So he proposed a series of constitutional amendments to make the plan affordable for the city by passing much of the funding on to the state. Many state legislators, however, were incensed to think that the state should be responsible for upwards of $5 million in improvements to one city, even if it was the capital.[192]

Despite the indifferent and unfriendly reception to his work, not to mention his brusque dismissal, Nolen remained charitably disposed toward Madison. When he returned to Madison in 1934 for the dedication of the UW Arboretum, one of his many recommendations, Nolen confessed his "love for Madison" and his continued friendships with many of Madison's most prominent citizens.[193]

Nolen's plan did not fade away. Instead, the concepts lodged themselves in the city's subconscious, slowly coming to the surface in the ensuing decades as Madison dared to dream what it could become.

Among the first of Nolen's recommendations to come to fruition was the expansion of the University of Wisconsin by five hundred acres. The city created the Madison City Plan Commission in 1920, and in 1923, the Wisconsin Supreme Court upheld a 1921 state law that limited the height of buildings on the Capitol Square, just as Nolen wanted. Madison received state approval to fill in Lake Monona to create a park in 1927, the same spot where Nolen had located his Grand Esplanade connecting the capitol to the lake. That same year, the city adopted its first zoning ordinance. In 1931, the city took control of all city parks from the Madison Park and Pleasure Drive Association and gave them to a newly created city park commission. The State Street Mall Nolen proposed came about, in a slightly altered form, in the 1970s.[194]

While many residents could push Nolen's criticisms from their mind, several other uncomfortable truths were harder to ignore: most notably, the deplorable conditions in which many residents found themselves living. Madison did have many beautiful homes, but it also had shacks and slums. The Latin Quarter between the campus, University Avenue and Henry Streets, and the Greenbush neighborhood were among the city's worst areas, crowded and unsanitary. Many other homes and apartment buildings were simply unsafe, crowded onto city lots to take advantage of city utilities and to house the growing population but without adequate fire escapes.[195]

In 1916, Lawrence Veiller, a nationally known housing expert and secretary of the National Housing Association, visited Madison and blasted the city for its terrible conditions. "You've got as bad a slum as any city in the country—worse than the slums of New York and Chicago," he said. "The people in Greenbush live in a dump with the most sordid outlook and surroundings I have ever seen."[196] The author of a model housing and tenement law, Veiller strongly advocated for urban renewal, explicitly evoking Nolen when he said that Madison could still be a model city through quick action.

The city responded slowly. Madison began regulating housing in 1913, passing a building code covering safety and sanitation, and hired the city's first full-time building inspector.[197] Requirements and standards tightened as the years went on, particularly after 1920, when Madison's first planning commission was created, one of Nolen's primary recommendations for the city's future welfare.

Madison also encouraged residents to move out of downtown and to the suburbs. Suburbs had arisen around Madison in the 1890s, first at Wingra Park and then at University Heights, offering more affordable housing to a growing population. Cities around the country had become more congested, making outlying areas attractive options for relieving urban pressures. The lack of transportation options from these suburbs to downtown had limited growth, however, as many residents were unwilling to walk more than one or two miles to work. The advent of streetcars, buses and, later, automobiles in the early twentieth century helped to loosen the tether between home and work, allowing more people to live farther from the city center.

Between 1903 and 1918, Madison annexed more than one thousand acres of suburban land, adding more people, taxable land and higher-quality homes to the city, three things the city desperately wanted.[198] In return, suburban dwellers got water and sewer systems, police and fire protection, schools and sidewalks, advantages that suburbs wanted but often could not afford.

At the same time that the city pushed people out, it also began filling in marshes and lake bottoms to create more space within the city. Developers could radically increase the value of their unused marshy land by filling it in. The filled areas created new buildable land and relieved Madison of some of its congestion. Unfortunately, some developers continued to pack buildings on tiny lots and to mix homes with factories.

All in all, Madison's attempts to improve housing quality did not immediately correct the serious housing problems in the most crowded areas of the city, particularly in the Latin Quarter and Greenbush. City leaders relied heavily on the suburbs and the automobile to create better housing for many decades.

Leaders were more successful in cleaning up the city and improving public health. Pressurized water and the underground network of laterals, collectors and mains allowed Madison residents to transport human waste safely and hygienically for the first time in the city's history by the early twentieth century. Before then, those without water closets dumped their chamber pots on the ground or in the streets, creating smelly piles of waste all over the city.[199]

Water closets had really been no better for the city, however, as many owners constructed private sewers that dumped their household waste directly into the lakes and marshes. Many doctors had warned that these marshy cesspools would become breeding grounds of disease. Finally, in 1885, the city moved forward on a district sewage system, acknowledging for the first time that the city held some responsibility for waste disposal.[200]

Unfortunately, that first city system deposited much of the waste into the lakes, too. An investigation of Madison's sanitary conditions on behalf of the local medical society in 1894 found the shorelines of Lakes Mendota and Monona coated in decaying fecal matter and the water filthy.[201] Something had to be done. Madison could not retain its image as a beautiful and healthy place with sewage-filled lakes.

Finally, after seeking the advice of countless experts and inspecting sewage systems in other cities, Madison got its first fairly effective sewage treatment plant in 1901. Over capacity within six years, the city had little option but to open a new sewage plant outside of the city. The new plant opened northwest of the city center in the town of Burke in 1917. In the decade between the time the old plant became obsolete and the new plant opened, more than three million gallons of partially treated sewage was dumped into

Lake Monona.[202] Even with the new plant, capacity remained a problem, and sewage continued to be pumped into the lake. Despite these problems in transporting and treating sewage completely and effectively, by 1920, privies were rare in Madison and indoor toilets the rule, lessening a major source of disease and filth.[203]

Besides sewers, Madison introduced other sanitary measures. City-funded garbage collection ended decades of unsanitary disposal practices. The filling of city marshes, once centers of disease, mosquitoes and smells, ended yet another health danger.

For those who still got sick despite Madison's beautification and health measures, the city finally got its first general hospital in 1903. Up until the 1880s, most healthcare happened at home. Health issues were private matters, and home was seen as the best place to receive care. In the late nineteenth century, a few private hospitals began offering care to those who could pay in Madison.

Madison General Hospital opened on October 15, 1903, at the intersection of Chandler and Mills Streets. Demand was so great that the hospital reached capacity less than a year after opening; an eighty-five-bed addition was added in 1912. The crowding of Madison General encouraged local Catholics to open their own hospital. St. Mary's Hospital opened in September 1911.[204] By 1920, Madison had eight hospitals, a startling growth in healthcare facilities in a short period of time that encouraged some city leaders to begin imagining Madison as a center of medicine.[205] The opening of Wisconsin General Hospital in 1924 (later the University of Wisconsin Hospital) allowed the University of Wisconsin to expand its medical training program from two to four years in 1925.

Making Madison a more beautiful, as well as more humane, city required a dramatic increase in government power in the early twentieth century. That this movement toward more public spaces and services achieved its full stride during the Progressive era was hardly surprising. Progressives favored government by experts, including planning professionals like John Nolen, and believed that cities should spend their money to improve the lives and living conditions of their people. It just sometimes took city leaders and residents a few years and several tries to get it right.

13

WORLD WAR I

War interrupted the Progressive era and strained Wisconsin's democratic traditions as the nations that many of the state's residents identified with squared off against one another in bloody conflict. American opinion about participation in the war was far from unanimous, even as official U.S. policy shifted from strict neutrality in 1914 toward the side of Great Britain by 1917.

The assassination of Austrian archduke Francis Ferdinand on June 28, 1914, did not immediately involve Madison residents and provoked war only between Austria and Serbia. But a tangled web of alliances between nations soon brought a dozen more countries and five million men into the fray, including German citizens living on the other side of the globe. The day after Germany invaded Belgium in August 1914, fifty Madison residents who still had German citizenship were ordered to return to Germany to take up arms.[206]

War did have an almost immediate effect on Madison's economy. Madison factories received orders for machinery, machine parts and other war supplies in the summer of 1914. In November 1914, residents sent thousands of pounds of cotton to Austria in response to Red Cross appeals for aid to wounded soldiers.[207]

With some of its residents fighting and some of its factories producing war supplies, Madison could scarcely remain neutral. The question of whether to support the Allies or the Central Powers was not easily resolvable, particularly for the city's German American community.

Still, most Madison residents managed to remain at least tolerant, if not completely neutral, of both sides. Even after the sinking of the British liner *Lusitania*, an act that killed more than one hundred Americans in May 1915, the *Wisconsin State Journal* reported that Madison citizens were giving generously to war relief efforts for both the Allies and the German-Austrian troops in 1916.

As the war dragged on, deteriorating conditions in Europe made American involvement seem all but imminent. In 1916, President Woodrow Wilson was reelected president largely because, as the slogan went, "He kept us out of war." Sixty-seven percent of Madison voters cast their ballots for Wilson and his message of neutrality.[208] Events in 1917 changed that. Frustrated over the British naval blockade, Germany resumed unrestricted submarine warfare in January 1917, sinking three American ships in March. In response, the United States severed diplomatic relations with Germany.

In late February, President Wilson learned of a telegram from German foreign minister Arthur Zimmermann to the German minister to Mexico offering Mexico the opportunity to reclaim its former territories in the southwestern United States in exchange for joining the German cause. No longer was the war over there. On April 6, 1917, the United States formally declared war on Germany and its allies.

With the declaration of war, neutrality was no longer an option in Madison, though support for the war was far from unanimous. Madison's sizable German American population, as well as its politically dominant Progressive party, including Senator Robert La Follette, generally opposed American entry into the war. German Americans maintained a strong cultural unity based on pride in German accomplishments, making it difficult for many of them to choose sides.

Senator Robert La Follette's opposition to the war was straightforward, if extremely controversial nationally. Although La Follette had supported President Wilson's election and reelection, he never strayed from Wilson's declared policy of strict neutrality from 1914. He argued that nothing in the aims and arguments of the belligerents on either side could possibly concern Americans enough to justify their participation. La Follette also worried that America's involvement in war would end democratic reforms at home. Reviled as a traitor, La Follette was burned in effigy, threatened with expulsion from the U.S. Senate and censured by more than four hundred UW staff members, who signed a statement charging him with aiding

Germany.[209] Nonetheless, La Follette's opposition did not end his political career, as he was reelected to the Senate in 1922.

The declaration of war unleashed a particularly virulent form of anti-German hysteria among Americans. Dissent of any kind led to accusations of treason. President Wilson's Committee on Public Information abetted the patriotic fervor by producing a rush of press releases, fliers, films and other loyalty campaigns aimed at shoring up support for the Allied cause. Many Madison residents were acutely sensitive to charges of disloyalty due to the publicity surrounding La Follette's opposition and the city's large German American population. *The Capital Times* was denied membership in the Board of Commerce in 1917 because of its support of La Follette.[210]

Unsurprisingly, German culture became suspect, and anyone or anything with a German name became a target for harassment. Madison's German-American Bank was forced to change its name after a January 12, 1918 letter in the *Wisconsin State Journal* questioned the bank's loyalty. German language teachers were also targeted. Madison public schools cut German language instruction from elementary schools, and enrollment in German classes at the university dropped from 1,400 students in 1917 to just 265 in 1918.[211] Additionally, all Madison residents over the age of fourteen born in Germany but not yet American citizens had to register as enemy aliens and carry ID cards. These enemy aliens were forbidden from coming within a half mile of the Forest Products Laboratory, ordnance works and any other war-related operation.[212]

German Americans responded variously to the attacks on their culture. While the easy course for many was to acquiesce to the outcry against everything German, others found it difficult to deny a heritage of which they felt quite proud.

Despite many sources of outspoken opposition, the majority of Madison residents did support the war. Brass bands and cheering crowds saw the first 150 Madison men off to war only a month after war was declared. Those who stayed at home bought more than $1.5 million in Liberty Loan bonds to support the war effort.[213]

These efforts were only the beginning, however. The first draft call was issued in July 1917, followed by a second Liberty Loan drive in October. The second draft call in April 1918 inaugurated what became monthly drafts thereafter. The third Liberty Loan drive launched in April 1918 and a fourth, in September. Liberty Loan committees organized in nearly all sections of

University of Wisconsin student cadets learn how to repair automobiles and trucks during World War I. *Wisconsin Historical Society Image ID #40911.*

the country to canvass as many people as possible. Four-minute speakers gave direct sales pitches to citizens in theaters, movie theaters, hotels and restaurants, and ministers made pleas from the pulpit for parishioners to purchase war bonds.[214]

The outbreak of war brought tremendous shortages of food and fuel across Europe as farm fields and factories became battlegrounds. By the time the United States entered the war in 1917, three years of fighting had seriously damaged European prewar trade routes and supplies. The Allies had come to depend on the productivity of the United States for food and supplies, so continuing to supply the Allies and fielding troops in Europe placed a tremendous strain on the U.S. economy. To help, Madison residents joined in national drives to conserve food and fuel.

As an agricultural state, Wisconsin took a special interest in the wartime food crisis. Wisconsin organized the nation's first State Council of Defense on April 12, 1917, and named Madison resident Magnus Swenson as chairman. The council's purpose was to educate citizens about the causes of war, to advise on efficient methods of functioning within a wartime economy and to identify those not doing their part to support the soldiers.

In his role as chair, Swenson quickly implemented programs to eliminate food waste and to conserve wheat, fat, sugar and meat. Madison residents stopped eating beef on Tuesdays, wheat on Wednesdays and pork on Saturdays, an eating plan soon adopted nationally. Women learned to feed their families rye, corn, chicken, fish and other perishable foods, so that more meat, fat and sugar could be sent abroad.[215]

To help them, the Women Students' War Work Council, together with the University of Wisconsin's Home Economics Department, produced a wartime recipe booklet in 1917 that used alternative, non-rationed ingredients. Recipes included steamed barley pudding, scalloped cheese, "salmon box" and rice croquettes.[216] Not to be outdone, the Woman's Committee of the Dane County Council of Defense published its own *Manual of Wheatless Recipes*, which sold more than eighteen thousand copies by the summer of 1918.[217]

Every household in the city was expected to display a card pledging its commitment to the war on food waste. Those who failed to display the sign risked being visited by members of the Woman's Committee, which patrolled city neighborhoods looking for holdouts. Women also created window displays in Madison storefronts, believing them the best means to advertise and educate women on food conservation. These were not just simple cardboard displays, though; Dane County Woman's Committee chair Mrs. L.M. Hobbins hired architects and designers from the University of Wisconsin to help with the design. One featured Mother Goose and the rhyme: "Sing a song of thrift stamps / A pocket full of rye / Flour and twenty Hoover kinds / Of bread and cake and pie."[218] Nearly every Madison household planted victory gardens and canned vegetables and fruits. Those without yards could garden on vacant city lots.

Federal authorities also issued orders to cut back on coal consumption. In January 1918, all Madison factories closed for five days. "Heatless Mondays" followed as factories, stores, shops and theaters closed for ten consecutive Mondays. Residents also traded the hard, smokeless coal for the soft, sootier kind so that navy ships would be less visible at sea.[219]

Resource conservation was not Madison's only contribution to the war. Local companies received governmental contracts for the production of machine tools, gas masks, batteries and other war goods.[220] The government also constructed two ordnance plants in Madison. The Northwest Ordnance Company opened on East Washington Avenue next to the Gisholt Machine Company and made guns and other armaments.[221] The other, the Four Lakes Ordnance Company, produced navy guns. Madison also contributed war-related research. The Forest Products Laboratory, a major USDA research center opened in 1910, found a way to reduce the drying time for gunstock and airplane woods and conducted crucial testing of woods, glues and lamination processes. C.F. Burgess Laboratories researched chemical warfare and produced batteries through its subsidiary, Burgess Battery Company. University faculty did everything from investigating mineral supplies and chemical warfare to preparing wartime propaganda.[222]

Even before America entered the war, peace groups were already hard at work in Wisconsin developing plans to end the war. One of the most noteworthy proposals to stop the fighting in Europe was developed by Julia Grace Wales, a young English professor at the University of Wisconsin. Deeply troubled by the reports of the brutal conflict, Wales formulated a plan to stop the evils of war without violence, a plan that the Wisconsin Peace Society printed and circulated under the title *Continuous Mediation Without Armistice* in 1915. The plan called for the United States to organize a conference of intellectuals from neutral nations who would act as mediators for the warring nations to arrive at a settlement.

The plan provoked immediate and overwhelmingly positive responses. Wales's proposal became known as the Wisconsin Plan, and within months, Wales was in the Netherlands, where the International Congress of Women unanimously selected the Wisconsin Plan as the solution to the war. Although some government officials seemed interested in Wales's proposal, the sinking of the *Lusitania* and the return of submarine warfare led officials to back away from mediation as a viable solution.[223]

American entry into the war helped the Allies launch major offenses that broke the stalemate on the front lines. But just as the tides of war appeared to be turning toward the Allies in the summer of 1918, disaster struck at home. The Spanish flu, one of the worst health epidemics in history, brought terror and devastation to people in Wisconsin and around the world. What appeared, at first, like a typical flu began turning deadly with increasing frequency. The flu came on quickly and without warning, rapidly overtaking healthy people and killing more young adults than people in any other age group.

The spread of flu coupled with anxiety over the war and fears of German American disloyalty proved to some residents that immigration should be restricted and alcohol prohibited for the sake of public health. Some thought that the mixing of people left homeless and adrift by the war would spread disease. Others blamed the Germans. Some feared that the continued arrival of immigrants would jeopardize American health. Prohibitionists argued that the gathering of people in saloons encouraged the spread of the disease.[224]

Madison's first flu cases were reported in October 1918, though health authorities were reluctant to identify it as the same deadly strain killing thousands of people around the world. Then came Madison's first deaths. Newspapers began printing the names of the dead, as many as ten a day. The State Board of Health, created in 1876, together with local public heath officials, responded to the health crisis with one of the best influenza control programs in the country. Health authorities closed schools and banned nearly all activities that brought large numbers of people together, including church, movies and plays. These uniform, statewide measures reduced the number of flu-related deaths and earned Wisconsin one of the lowest death rates in the country. Even so, 268 Madison residents died from the flu.[225]

Finally, on November 11, 1918, Madison residents learned that an armistice had been signed and the war was over. Church bells, factory whistles and honking car horns greeted the news. About twelve thousand celebrants met at the square and marched to Camp Randall.[226]

Madison's soldiers did not return immediately from Europe; ninety Madison men never came back. The United States had only a limited number of ships with which to transport more than two million men home. Not until May 1919 did most of Madison's soldiers return aboard a special train. Nearly twenty thousand Madison residents turned out to greet the train and escort the men to the capitol for a ceremony.[227]

In the Senate, La Follette opposed the Versailles Treaty ending the war and American membership in the League of Nations. He saw the treaty as a violation of Wilson's pledges and the League of Nations as an organization for victors only. The United States never joined the League of Nations.

As happy as everyone was to have the war over and the soldiers home, the transition from war to peace was anything but easy. Factories that had expanded capacity to meet wartime demands now cut back, leaving hundreds of Madison workers without jobs. With war-inflated building prices still in effect, builders refused to risk having to sell their products at deflated postwar prices, creating a backlog of five hundred homes. As a result, rental prices soared, and vacancy rates reached new lows.[228]

One bright spot was the diminishment of anxiety over the loyalty of German Americans as Madison residents looked ahead to a world changed by war.

14

PROSPERITY AND DEPRESSION

When World War I ended, many Madison residents anticipated a return to peaceful daily pursuits. And the decade did bring new prosperity and hope to many as daily life was dramatically altered by new scientific and technological innovation. Madison's businesses saw much positive change. Fancy new stores lined downtown streets, turning Madison into a regional shopping hub. But this new prosperity did not come without anxiety and some conflict.

The Capitol Square acquired new buildings for government, business and tourism, including the fancy Hotel Loraine and the more utilitarian Belmont Hotel in 1924. The Belmont Hotel was Madison's tallest building, at eleven stories, when it opened, a full fifteen feet above the one-hundred-foot height limit imposed by the legislature for buildings on the square.[229] Among the square's other new buildings were a post office, a U.S. Courthouse and two headquarters buildings for Wisconsin Power and Light and the Beaver Insurance Company. In 1929, a new $1 million federal building opened, the first of several government buildings that would grace the mall area John Nolen had called for linking the capitol to the lake. The legislature also authorized the construction of a large office annex to the capitol, the first wing of which was completed at 1 West Wilson in 1932.[230]

The opening of three new theaters kept residents entertained and helped turn State Street into Madison's entertainment district. The Orpheum Theatre opened on March 21, 1927, paid for in part by dentist William

Beecroft, known locally as "Mr. Theater" for his love of movies and live entertainment. Its French Renaissance exterior and Art Deco limestone exterior made it one of the most fashionable public spaces in town. One year later, on January 21, 1928, the opulent Capitol Theatre opened across the street, designed by renowned Chicago architects Rapp & Rapp. The theater had a Moorish Spanish theme and boasted the latest in modern conveniences and technology for both movie and vaudeville performances. It also had a Grand Barton theater organ constructed by the Barton Musical Instrument Company of Oshkosh. Away from downtown, the Eastwood Theatre, today known as the Barrymore, opened on December 27, 1929. The Eastwood was the state's first theater with a built-in movie sound system.

The 1920s saw the growth of two major Madison companies as well. The French Battery Company, maker of dry cell batteries, began in Madison in 1906. World War I had been profitable for the firm, which sold batteries for military radios, and within a few years, Madison stood at the forefront of battery production in the United States. One of the city's largest employers by the 1920s, the French Battery Company renamed itself Ray-O-Vac in 1934.

Another major Madison employer to emerge was Oscar Mayer and Company. Five thousand area farmers formed the Farmers' Cooperative Packing Company in 1914 and opened a packing plant next to the city sewage treatment center in May 1917. Despite opening during the war, the plant managed to survive the challenging times, only to fall victim to the labor unrest that followed the war in 1919. The plant closed and went up for sale.

Oscar G. Mayer learned of the plant's sale while visiting his in-laws in Madison. Mayer, general manager and secretary of his father's Chicago packing plant, agreed to purchase the site in July 1919 and hired Adolph C. Bolz to run the operation. To help his employees get to work, Mayer agreed to subsidize the extension of the streetcar tracks to the plant. He also constructed fifty affordable homes near the plant for workers.

The new Oscar Mayer and Company was a near-instant success, with sales reaching $2 million in 1922. The company's workforce grew from 250 in 1919 to 400 by 1929, and despite the Depression, employment tripled in the next decade. By its thirty-fifth anniversary in 1954, Oscar Mayer employed more than 4,500 workers, nearly a third of the city's entire industrial workforce.

All of these good times did not come without significant troubles, however. The postwar depression, while short, brought considerable hardship to Wisconsin workers. Wage cuts and job losses led to a series of strikes, most unsuccessful, including the Madison Strike of 1919. The strike began when employers proved unwilling to honor the concessions recently won by workers: an eight-hour workday, time-and-a-half pay for overtime, an end to piecework, collective bargaining and equal pay for women.[231] With no enforcement provisions, though, employers simply ignored them.

On April 1, 1919, twenty-five hundred workers walked off the job. The carpenters union joined the strike two days later. Five days later, on April 8, nearly two thousand striking workers and supporters marched on the Capitol Square as the legislature debated an eight-hour-day bill that was eventually defeated. Worker unrest continued to grow as more unions voted to strike in reaction to employer inaction. But time and again, despite government backing for worker rights, the agreements had no teeth, so employers continued to refuse to honor the rights of their employees. This staunch refusal eventually broke the back of the unions, and the striking workers went back to work. Organized labor did not begin to recover in Madison until the 1930s.[232]

Prohibition proved just as difficult to enforce as to pass. Although a majority of Madison residents voted for Prohibition, many remained skeptical of how effectively it would curb drinking from the beginning, even more so with widespread reports of crime and lawlessness throughout the state. Prohibition left a huge consumer market for alcohol unmet by legal means. Organized crime helped to fill the gap but also brought increased violence.

In 1929, Herbert Hoover appointed George Wickersham to head a commission charged with making recommendations for improving the enforcement and administration of federal laws. His official report contained a section on Wisconsin suggesting that Prohibition violations were more common than some people wanted to believe.

In Madison, investigator Frank Buckley visited the Greenbush neighborhood. There he found "an attractive young Italian girl," known as "the queen of the bootleggers," who "catered exclusively to fraternity house clientele." Buckley likely encountered Jennie Justo, who was jailed in 1933 for allegedly running a speakeasy at 921 Spring Street. She certainly was not the only one with alcohol in the neighborhood. In November 1922, the police seized 475 gallons of wine in raids along Regent Street.

Some people had secret stills in their basements that were only discovered when they exploded.

At the University of Wisconsin, Buckley talked with the assistant dean of women, who claimed that the young ladies in her care did not drink. Buckley did not buy her story, however; he thought her naïve if she actually believed that college students were not breaking the law.[233]

Despite amassing a wealth of material, the members of the Wickersham Commission could not agree on a plan of action to amend the Prohibition enforcement laws. Wisconsin residents, on the other hand, came up with their own solution. In 1929, voters repealed the state's Prohibition enforcement law. Wisconsin senator John J. Blaine, pledging loyalty to the will of the people, proposed a constitutional amendment for the repeal of Prohibition. The U.S. Senate modified Blaine's resolution and passed the measure without delay. The Twenty-first Amendment was ratified on December 5, 1933, and national Prohibition ended.

Madison residents celebrate the end of Prohibition at the Fauerbach Brewery tavern in 1933. *Wisconsin Historical Society Image ID #3493.*

Violence associated with drinking was not the only thing residents feared following the war—they also feared each other. During World War I, many people worried about German American disloyalty. That fear generally dissipated after the war, but a lingering fear of subversive ideas and groups remained. The triumph of the Bolsheviks in Russia only aggravated that concern and led many Americans to worry about the spread of communism to the United States. But rather than seize radical organizers as they did in other parts of the country, major efforts in Wisconsin to control radicalism continued to focus, instead, on making immigrants and other ethnic groups more American, an approach to social reform with roots in the late nineteenth century.

Settlement houses offered one method of Americanization. Often located in crowded immigrant neighborhoods, settlement houses provided services and classes to the poor and newly arrived immigrants. Madison got its first settlement house in 1916 with the opening of Neighborhood House in the Greenbush neighborhood. Serving primarily Italians, whom many Madison residents thought needed the most "Americanizing," Neighborhood House workers tried to ease the adjustment to living in a new country by consciously teaching white, middle-class values through educational offerings in everything from English, health and cooking to sewing and citizenship.[234]

World War I only intensified the Americanization crusade in Madison. Immigrants learned how to be more American from hundreds of volunteers that included everyone from university students to members of the Ku Klux Klan. These citizenship efforts continued after the war, but with hysteria over communism and Bolshevism, these efforts took a new and ugly twist.

Worried about the influence of immigrants, some residents began calling for immigration restrictions, the deportation of aliens and the elimination of foreign-language courses in schools in favor of strict English-only usage. In June 1919, the *Wisconsin State Journal* demanded that the legislature take on "this vital American issue" to make Wisconsin "a 100 per cent American state."[235]

In this uneasy atmosphere, the Ku Klux Klan found fertile ground to plant their fiery crosses. The Klan first appeared in Wisconsin in the fall of 1920, near Milwaukee. One year later, an ad in the *Wisconsin State Journal* calling for 100 percent American men between the ages of twenty-four and forty to join a "fraternal order" was later revealed to have been placed by the Klan. In October 1924, the Klan staged its first parade in Madison,

Ku Klux Klan members parade down King Street in Madison in 1924. *Wisconsin Historical Society Image ID #1902.*

drawing a sizable crowd to watch the white-hooded spectacle. Soon after, Klan insignia began appearing around town.

The Klan gained power in Madison by promising to maintain order in Greenbush, an area rocked by violence and illegal alcohol in the 1920s. Eager to attract new members, it was a logical choice for the Klan, as Madison lacked sizable populations of any of the Klan's typical list of enemies.[236]

To help the Klan, Mayor Milo Kittleson and E.H. Drews, president of Madison's Police and Fire Commission, secretly deputized thirty Klansmen to conduct raids in Greenbush, paid for by the mayor's office. Rather than be condemned for his secret actions, however, Kittleson was later reimbursed for his expenses.

The Klan's ascendancy in Madison was short-lived, however, declining not long after it first appeared. With little long-term benefits to offer members and no clear statement of purpose, the Klan was unable to maintain member loyalty and support. The last major Klan event in Dane County was held in the fall of 1925, and the Klan had all but disappeared from Wisconsin by 1928. Two decades later, in December 1946, circuit court judge Herman Sachtjen revoked the Klan's state charter on the grounds that it served no legal purpose and that the group stood for principles contrary to American values.

Despite the troubles of the decade, many Madison residents continued to feel optimistic about the future. With economic conditions reasonably good, few people took precautions to avert another depression. Many people hoped that the horrors of war were behind them and that peace and prosperity would continue indefinitely.

The stock market crash came as a surprise to many. On October 29, 1929, many more investors tried to sell stock than tried to buy new shares. Stock prices tumbled far below what investors had paid, and within hours, people who owned great wealth on paper were unable to pay back their loans. Many tried to sell stock to raise cash, only lowering prices further; in only ninety days, the stock market lost 40 percent of its value, and $26 billion of wealth disappeared.

In Madison, people turned from sneaking bootleg alcohol to devising ways to survive the worst depression in the nation's history. Factories closed, wages dropped and unemployment swelled.

Madison fared slightly better than other towns and cities with its many university and state employees. *The Capital Times* reported that the state treasurer was paying $300,000 monthly in salaries to more than two thousand state employees, most of whom lived in Madison, in December 1930. A store executive told *Capital Times* editor William T. Evjue, "You don't know what the depressions is. You should see the situation in such factory towns as Akron and Ft. Wayne."[237] Even so, Madison's unemployment rate had risen to 16 percent by April 1931, almost mirroring the national average. More than thirty-four hundred Madison residents found themselves out of work.

Efforts by policymakers to overcome economic stagnation took place in an atmosphere of intense social conflict. Extremists from across the political spectrum, from communists on the left to fascists on the right, thought they understood who was to blame for the current catastrophe and what should be done to fix it. Certain in their own viewpoints and anxious about the future, many felt justified in using force to try to bring about their goals.

One group that experienced renewed militancy was organized labor. In March 1930, about thirty unemployed men and two women marched into Madison's city hall and issued thirteen demands to Mayor Albert Schmedeman. Responding to their query on what he intended to do for the thousands of jobless workers, Schmedeman responded, "What can I do? What power do you think I have to create work?"[238] Three days later, Schmedeman did what little he could, announcing the hiring of eighty men for street and sewer repairs two months earlier than planned.[239]

Dissatisfied with official responses to unemployment, the Madison chapter of the National Trade Union Unity League, an industrial union founded by the Communist Party of the United States in 1929, decided to stage another demonstration a few days later. It chose March 6, 1930, to hold its march, the day the Communist Party had selected as International Unemployment Day.

On the day of the demonstration, the protestors marched toward the capitol. Reaching the Capitol Square, the protesters were met by an angry crowd of university students who blamed the union and the Communists for the nation's economic crisis. Led by five university athletes, the students manhandled the protesters, tore their banners and scattered their pamphlets on the streets. Although the students were arrested for their actions, they were not the only Madison residents to believe that radicals were responsible for the severity of the Depression.[240]

Even before President Franklin Roosevelt's New Deal started to bring some relief in the mid-1930s, the Wisconsin legislature enacted relief programs of its own, including the nation's first unemployment compensation law. University of Wisconsin economist John R. Commons had promoted unemployment compensation for two decades, but the bill he wrote was repeatedly introduced without success during the prosperous 1920s. As the Depression worsened and more people lost their jobs, however, public opinion changed, and a new unemployment bill, drafted by UW economist and assemblyman Harold Groves, finally passed in early 1932, becoming a model for the nation.

Seeing its success, President Roosevelt appointed UW economists Arthur Altmeyer and Edwin Witte to serve on the Committee on Economic Security in 1934. After studying the unemployment and pension programs of other nations, Witte and Altmeyer devised a program that established a national retirement-age insurance system, federal-state unemployment insurance and aid to dependent mothers and others who could not work. The federal government extended protection to the unemployed, the aged and the disabled with the passage of the Social Security Act in 1935.

That same year, 1935, Roosevelt authorized the Works Progress Administration (WPA) to put out-of-work Americans to work on public projects. In Madison, WPA workers built sewers and water pipes and constructed buildings. WPA draftsmen drew street and utility maps that engineers still check regularly for information on sewers, water mains and even the building materials on old streets. Much of Madison's original airport, including a massive stone hangar still in use as a storage building, was built by WPA workers. Workers also built a breakwater in Lake Mendota at Tenney Park, restored some of Madison's Indian mounds and removed abandoned streetcar tracks. Some of the most visible WPA structures still in use today are the restrooms, shelters and fireplaces at Hoyt Park, built by skilled Italian workmen.

The WPA did not just create manual labor jobs, though; it also created jobs for white-collar workers and for those in the performing and fine arts. Artists left striking murals on post offices, schools and other public buildings. Artist James Watrous painted a sprawling scene of Paul Bunyan and his folktale world in the Memorial Union on the UW campus. Writers prepared state and regional guidebooks, organized archives and conducted historical and sociological investigations.

Another work relief program, the Civilian Conservation Corps (CCC), put unemployed young men to work on conservation projects on local, state and federal lands. They built ranger stations, picnic shelters, restrooms, bridges and hiking trails in parks. In Madison, CCC workers camped at the new UW Arboretum and began work never done anywhere in the world before: the purposeful restoration of a prairie.[241] The camp, which stayed open until the start of World War II, was the only one of its kind on a university campus. CCC crews worked with botanists Norman Fassett, John T. Curtis and John Thomson to collect, propagate and nurture prairie vegetation. The work began in Curtis Prairie, which remains today the arboretum's flagship restoration project, inspiring restoration efforts around the world.

The government was not the only one to offer programs to help people get through hard times. The Madison Vocational and Adult School, today's MATC, increased its craft offerings in the 1930s, scheduling classes in millinery, woodworking and chair caning. Finding new areas of education helped the college survive the Depression at a time when community colleges around the United States closed.

Roosevelt's success on the national level helped to temporarily discredit the Republican Party and led Wisconsin Progressives, particularly Governor Phil La Follette, son of Robert La Follette, and his brother, Senator Robert

La Follette Jr., to organize a separate Progressive Party in 1934. The first of two organizing meetings of the new party was held in Madison in March 1934. The new party called for an improved conservation program, the distribution of milk as a public utility, the initiative and referendum on the national level and a popular referendum on war—the last was a vestige of Progressive opposition to the First World War. Both La Follettes ran under the slogan "Run with the La Follettes and win," and win they did, because when the votes were counted, the Progressives controlled the state legislature and sent seven men to Congress.

Although New Deal policies and programs reduced the suffering of many Madison residents, it was the country's entrance into World War II that finally brought the economy back to health.

15

WORLD WAR II

The outbreak of the Second World War ushered in a period of great prosperity and unity in Wisconsin. Unlike World War I, antiwar sentiment virtually ended with the United States' entry into the war. There was no crusading antiwar enthusiasm or strong opposition minority. Although Senator Robert La Follette Jr. and Governor Phil La Follette opposed American involvement in the war, upholding the legacy of their father, both recognized, like most Wisconsin residents, that Nazi victories and the threat of fascism justified U.S. participation and so muted their criticisms. Residents also had come to recognize that their German and Italian neighbors bore no responsibility for the conduct of their home nations and that there was a difference between fanatics and ordinary civilians.

With the coming of war, the Depression years receded into the background as defense spending and military preparedness resulted in defense contracts for Wisconsin businesses. Rather than the dismal employment prospects that plagued the 1930s, labor was in high demand, and wages and prices rose accordingly.

As Madison shifted to wartime production, city businesses became more dependent on orders from the military than ever before. The Badger Ordnance Works just north of Madison quickly grew into one of the largest manufacturers of ammunition in the world. Opened in 1942, Badger Ordnance provided employment for seventy-five hundred workers during the war. Many of those workers lived in the complex of barracks-like housing on the site known as Badger Village. After the war, Badger Village became temporary housing for veterans attending the University of Wisconsin on the GI Bill.[242] Other Madison factories turned out machine tools and heavy machinery for the war. Ray-O-Vac manufactured batteries for walky-talkies, producing more than 300,000 a day.[243]

Expanded demand for labor created housing shortages in Madison. Housing shortages usually occurred in places where wartime production attracted workers from afar. By March 1942, Madison had joined several Wisconsin communities designated as "critical defense housing" areas. This status made it easier for Madison to acquire scarce building materials, to receive loans for rehabilitation or new construction and to take part in federally funded housing projects.[244]

To help train workers for the wartime jobs, the federal government provided funding for "national defense" courses. The Madison Vocational and Adult School, today's Madison Area Technical College, offered courses twenty-four hours a day during the 1942–43 school year. Third-shift courses focused in particular on manufacturing skills, allowing men to work day jobs while learning new skills at night. Other programs incorporated wartime subjects into the traditional curriculum. Homemaking, for example, added classes in "Consumer Interests in Wartime" and "Children in Wartime."[245]

Thousands of soldiers took classes, too, taking advantage of correspondence courses offered by the University of Wisconsin. The courses were often administered through the United States Armed Forces Institute.

While industrial work provided one of the most valuable ways for civilians to aid the war effort, most of the available men who would have otherwise worked in these factories were needed on the battlefield once the United States joined the war.

So factories turned to women to replace many of the men who joined the armed forces, opening doors to women that women's rights advocates had been unable to budge through other means. Madison women went right to work, processing hot dogs at Oscar Mayer and building batteries at Ray-O-Vac.[246] Ammunitions maker Madison-Kipp lost 365 male employees to the war and was even forced to halt certain production lines when all of the men working that line were drafted. To make up for the shortfall and then some, Madison-Kipp hired hundreds of women as the workforce swelled to 1,500 workers to meet wartime demands.[247] Jean Larsen became one of only 3

Women took on many jobs during World War II, including processing hot dogs at Oscar Mayer. *Wisconsin Historical Society Image ID #34559.*

female projectionists in the country when she began working the projector at the University of Wisconsin Memorial Union Play Circle. Before the war, only men had held this position.[248]

Women who worked in factories encountered many problems never faced by the men they replaced. Those with children needed childcare, which was often expensive. This was particularly problematic, as women also received less pay than male workers with the same or even less experience.

The opportunities for women provided by the war did not last, however. Hundreds of women lost their jobs as early as 1944, a trend that only continued as the war drew to a close. The job market, inflated by wartime production, could not employ both women and returning veterans. Some women left the labor force permanently, while others found different work in the postwar economy. Even with the voluntary and involuntary layoffs, though, more women remained in the labor force than ever before.[249]

Besides women, high school students also provided temporary labor to make up for the shortages. A work-credit program allowed students to divide their days between school and work around town. Madison students did everything from load bread trucks for the Gardner Baking Company to helping with the wash at the Quality Service Laundry.[250]

The Madison Municipal Airport also shifted to war work when it was activated as an Army Air Force airfield in 1942. Renamed Truax Field in honor of Wisconsin-native Lieutenant Thomas L. Truax, who was killed in a training accident in November 1941, the field served as a major training center for radio operators, mechanics and other communication operations. Truax Field was deactivated as an active military base in 1968, when it was taken over by the Wisconsin Air National Guard.

Unlike previous wars, the vast majority of Wisconsin men and women served in units having no particular association with the state. They volunteered or were drafted and were sent to training camps and bases in other states and assigned to units based on need. So many UW students enlisted that enrollment dropped by half.

At least 150 university faculty members provided research and other assistance for problems of national defense, including E.B. Fred, who headed the nation's biological warfare research program and later became UW president. Three UW scientists also worked on the government's secret program to build the atomic bomb.

The university also established schools on campus for various training purposes. Schools for the navy included radio training, cooking and baking, training for navy air pilots and diesel engineering instruction for naval officers. Meteorological training and training for air force machinists was provided for the army. Additionally, the university Reserve Officer Training Corps (ROTC) organized the nation's first ski patrol.[251]

Over 330,000 Wisconsin citizens served, including 9,000 women who enlisted as nurses, parachute riggers, cryptographers, weather observers and ferry pilots. Each branch of the military had special units for women. They served in WAVES (Women Accepted for Volunteer Emergency Service), WAC (Women's Army Corps), Marines, WASP (Women Airforce Service Pilots) or SPARS (*Semper Paratus*—Always Ready). Approximately 8,000 Wisconsin men and women died; 330 were from Dane County.[252]

While some Madison residents left for service and others worked in war-related jobs, nearly everyone participated in the war effort at home. Until the war ended in August 1945, the daily challenges of wartime shortages of food, gasoline and other essential goods were a part of everyone's lives. Gasoline rationing began in 1942. Most drivers received four gallons a week, but this was later reduced to two. The government also instituted a national speed limit of thirty-five miles per hour to help conserve gas and the rubber in tires. Wisconsin's Consumer Interests Committee organized county-level consumer councils and organizations to educate people on basic cost- and product-saving measures. As in World War I, citizens were urged to plant gardens, preserve food and learn general home maintenance. Classes were organized, especially for women, in basic home and car repair. Citizens also participated in air raid drills and blackouts as the development of strategic bombing led to new forms of civilian defense.

For many people, the hardest wartime adjustment to make was the meat ration. Brats, roasts, steaks and assorted fish and fowl were staples in many Madison homes. By 1942, the meat ration was two and a half pounds per person per week. Black markets for meat and other rationed goods soon sprang up. Although the number of people who actually traded black market meat was unknown, the government believed it was enough of a concern to issue booklets warning about the dangers of underground meat.

Interestingly, one of the world's most distinguished string quartets found a new home in Madison during the war. Belgium's Pro Arte Quartet had come to Madison in May 1940 for a series of concerts, but Hitler's invasion of Belgium on May 10, 1940, left the musicians stranded in the United States. In response, the university offered the quartet a permanent home on campus. The group agreed and began holding weekly concerts, radio and television broadcasts and performances across Wisconsin, a tradition that continues to this day.[253]

After the war, enrollment at UW exploded as veterans took advantage of the GI Bill. The Campus Planning Commission approved the construction of twelve new buildings and the expansion of existing structures to house and educate all the students. Housing shortages forced students into metal huts, tents and trailers located on every open space on campus. Some faculty members even held class in local churches due to space constraints.

Once the war ended on September 2, 1945, people in Madison, as everywhere, wanted to put the war behind them and get on with their lives. But the war had changed the social and economic fabric of the city, state and country, and there would be no return to the past for veterans, workers, women and city dwellers.

16

CITY OF FEAR

After World War II, foreign affairs played a larger role than ever before in the lives of American citizens. The United States competed with the Union of Soviet Socialist Republics (USSR) for political and economic dominance around the world as part of the Cold War. This rivalry shaped nearly every aspect of international politics, as well as many domestic concerns, until the fall of the Berlin Wall in 1989 and the dissolution of the USSR in the 1990s.

In the late 1940s, people in Wisconsin were divided over issues such as the creation of the United Nations, support for European recovery and the growing power of the Soviet Union. But when postwar Europe divided into communist and capitalist powers, public opinion generally supported the protection of democracy and capitalism against communist expansion. That tension came to a head in Korea.

The Korean War has often been called America's forgotten war, though like Vietnam, it was part of a larger Cold War struggle to contain and extinguish communism. In 1950, North Korean communist troops invaded South Korea, which was an American ally. Seeking to protect South Korea and to prevent the spread of communism in Asia, President Harry Truman sent General Douglas MacArthur to command the United Nations forces. Lasting three years (1950–53), the Korean conflict was dominated by politically motivated negotiations and stalemates that delayed the armistice and cost thousands of lives.

Around 132,000 Wisconsin citizens served in Korea, the first armed confrontation of the Cold War. All able-bodied male students at UW had to enroll in two years of compulsory ROTC. After that, they could take two additional years of ROTC leading to a commission and active service, or they could take their chances on a semester-to-semester draft deferment.

Some, like Richard Hemlin of Madison, were drafted in 1952. Hemlin remembers feeling unprepared for war. "Everybody was hoping Eisenhower would come in and it was going to be over. I thought maybe I'd sail right through, and that didn't happen." Hemlin served in the army's Seventh Division.[254]

When hostilities ceased with the signing of the armistice on July 27, 1953, Chinese armies remained on their side of the North Korean border, and North and South Korea, separated by a wide "demilitarized zone" along the thirty-eighth parallel, entered a long period of tense relations that continues to this day.

Despite being overshadowed by World War II and Vietnam, Korea marked many firsts for the United States. Military units were officially racially integrated for the first time in American history. Korea created the idea of a "limited war," where two superpowers fight their battles in another country and where the objective is not the total destruction of the enemy. Korea also expanded the Cold War, which had, to that point, been mostly confined to Europe.

Because communism, in practice, tightened restrictions on personal freedom and allowed for government control of business, it seemed to threaten the American ideals of individual liberty and free enterprise. Communist expansion in Eastern Europe and Korea fueled Americans' anxiety that their way of life was under attack and launched the career of Wisconsin senator Joseph McCarthy.

After several uneventful years in the Senate, McCarthy made headlines when he announced in a February 9, 1950 speech in Wheeling, West Virginia, that he knew of 205 communists currently working in the State Department (he later reduced this number to 57). This wasn't the first time that McCarthy had raised the specter of communism—he had accused his Democratic opponent in the 1946 campaign of being a "little megaphone" for the communists, but to little effect, as communism was not yet a major national issue. But in 1950, as American men and women were preparing to sacrifice their lives in combat against a communist enemy in Korea, this speech garnered great publicity. Capitalizing on people's fears of encroaching communism, McCarthy launched a public campaign aimed at eliminating the supposed communist infiltration of government and foreign policy. His pronouncements catapulted him to national prominence and provided a strong platform for his reelection in 1952.

As chair of a Senate Permanent Investigations Subcommittee, McCarthy took it upon himself to expose communists and their sympathizers, not only in government, but also throughout all of American political and cultural life. Under his leadership, the subcommittee interrogated more than five hundred people. McCarthy's accusations were often unsubstantiated, but in a political and cultural climate filled with fear, they gave him considerable power.

Hiding behind the veil of national security, McCarthy and his staff often refused to reveal their sources of information at a time when simply being called before his committee could ruin an individual's career. Many leaders of labor unions and professional organizations joined in the Red Scare hysteria simply out of fear of being named communist sympathizers themselves. Some intellectuals, activists and Hollywood writers did refuse to answer McCarthy's questions or to appear before his committee, despite the threat to their personal well-beings, and were blacklisted by their employers for refusing to cooperate with the committee.

Even before McCarthy reached the national stage, Madison's *Capital Times* newspaper had been exposing his wrongdoings, first as a judge and then as a senator. Among the questionable practices reported by the paper were McCarthy's avoidance of paying income taxes on stock market earnings, his doctoring of his war record, his violations of the constitutional provision against running for political office while holding a judicial post and his use of his circuit court stationery to raise campaign funds. McCarthy accused the paper and its city editor Cedric Parker of following "the communist line down to the last period" in a speech to the Madison Shriners on November 11, 1949. His attack was met head-on with editorials, and newspaper staff signed a letter calling McCarthy's claims baseless.

In 1951, when most newspapers continued to unquestioningly report McCarthy's charges, Evjue went to Washington, D.C., to meet with President Harry Truman. Evjue warned the president and the Capitol press corps of McCarthy's record. The next day, McCarthy took to the floor of the Senate to denounce *The Capital Times*, which he had taken to calling the "Prairie Pravda."

In 1953, however, McCarthy went too far when he accused the army of harboring communists. Broadcast nationally, the hearings brought McCarthy's bullying tactics and unsupported charges into American living rooms. TV commentator Edward R. Murrow helped to successfully expose his tactics and publicly denounced his actions as a threat to Americans' core democratic values. McCarthy came under attack from another local source in 1954, when Leroy Gore, a Sauk City newspaper editor, launched a "Joe Must Go" recall campaign of McCarthy. Gore brought his message to Madison's Turner Hall shortly after starting his effort, assuring the cheering crowd that they had a real chance of success. Unfortunately, the challenge of gathering more than 400,000 signatures from registered voters proved too much for Gore, and his crusade failed. But only a few months later, in December 1954, the Senate officially rebuked McCarthy for "conduct unbecoming a senator."[255] This did not remove him from office, however, as some of his critics hoped, but it did greatly diminish his power.

Though only in power for a brief period, McCarthy attained worldwide recognition, symbolizing the frenetic anti-communism that gripped American foreign policy in the 1950s. Virtually unknown outside Wisconsin in 1950, McCarthy was politically destroyed by 1955; he died in 1957. During those five years of power, though, McCarthy was a hero and champion to those who believed that the country had lost its authority in the postwar years and an evil, dangerous man to those who believed he exploited fears and violated standards of honesty.

Fighting communism at home took many forms. The national Crusade for Freedom, a domestic public relations and media campaign against communism that lasted from 1950 to 1960, came to Madison in 1951. At a kickoff before a Badger football game at Camp Randall, Madison residents were urged to sign "freedom scrolls" pledging their support to those living in communist countries fighting against their "Kremlin masters." During the game, the UW band also formed an outline of the freedom bell, the symbol of the organization. Attorney Floyd Springer Jr. led the Madison chapter, which also collected money from residents and sponsored showings of anti-communist movies.[256]

Communist fear also drove Madison residents underground and under desks in the 1950s. After the first atomic bomb was dropped on Japan in 1945, Americans realized that a new era, one in which humans had the power to destroy the world, was now upon them. Fear of nuclear warfare and the adverse effects of atomic radiation pervaded popular film, literature and other forms of mass culture. Once the Soviets detonated their first atomic bomb in 1949, apprehension escalated, as many Americans now believed that at an atomic war was on the horizon and that they could be among the victims.

The federal government created the Federal Civil Defense Administration (later called the Office of Civil Defense) to instruct the public about how to prepare for a nuclear assault. Educational materials were given to families, and teachers taught children atomic attack survival techniques at school, including the famous "duck and cover" maneuver. Children also wore identification bracelets so their bodies could be identified in the debris.

Madison Girl Scouts prepared public programs on ways to prepare for emergencies at an event held at the Dane County Fairgrounds in 1960. One group constructed a model bomb shelter and exhibited the amount and type of food needed for seven days in hiding. The Scouts also displayed shelter plans created by the Federal Civil Defense Administration.[257]

The bomb or fallout shelter was the most common form of recommended protection. Most survival manuals assured people that they could emerge from their shelters and return to their normal lives in only two weeks. Public shelters staffed with trained volunteers and stocked with civil defense equipment and supplies opened in many government buildings. The shelter at the State Historical Society supposedly could shelter 605 people, though they should hope for a shorter time underground, as it did not have enough supplies for that many people. The shelter included a seventeen-gallon water-storage drum (to be reused as a toilet when empty), a medical kit, a sanitation kit and survival biscuits. Other shelters had Geiger counters to locate the presence of radiation. Shelter leaders were required to use portable radios to keep in touch with the local Civil Defense agency, which would keep people informed on what was happening above ground.

For those who could not afford to build a shelter, the Civil Defense Administration recommended that families fix up a corner of the basement with all the necessary survival supplies. The *Wisconsin State Journal* and *The Capital Times* frequently printed shelter plans and suggested supply lists, as well as the occasional story about mansion-like shelters built by movie stars and business moguls.

City officials also sent the pamphlet *Evacuation of Madison: What To Do* to every Madison resident in the early 1950s. Each neighborhood received a tailored version with clear, detailed instructions for evacuating in case of atomic attack.[258]

While Americans were bombarded with fearful images of atomic annihilation, they also saw the atom portrayed in positive and humorous ways. America's growing interest in all things atomic prompted manufacturers and other commercial businesses to use the atom symbol and the word "atomic" to capture public attention and to project images of progress and modernity. "Atomic," "nuclear" and "H-bomb" became slang terms used to signify things that were awesome or monumental. Americans also began laughing at some of their own atomic fears in movies and comic books.

New events and concerns drove the fear of nuclear war from the minds of many Americans by the mid-1960s. The Cuban missile crisis of October 1962 represented the peak of anxiety about nuclear war, but afterward the Soviet Union and the United States agreed to take the first steps toward nuclear disarmament. While this action allowed many Americans to breathe a sigh of relief, other concerns, such as the civil rights movement and the escalating Vietnam War, occupied center stage. At the same time, increased interest in the space race, which had started with the Soviet launching of the Sputnik satellite in 1959, made images of space exploration the new symbols of modern technology.

17

CIVIL RIGHTS

As the civil rights movement picked up strength in the 1950s, many Madison residents viewed the growing unrest over racial equality as a southern problem. Indeed, Madison had long seen itself as one of the best places for African Americans in the state. White and black residents could live together, work together, shop together and sit beside one another in movies and theaters. But as the civil rights movement spread northward in the 1960s, the injustices occurring beneath the shiny exterior became harder to ignore, and Madison residents were forced to confront their own brand of racial inequities.

African Americans first settled in Madison in the 1850s. Madison's first known black resident, William Noland, arrived in the 1850s from New York. His sons became the first African Americans born in Madison. Noland worked as a barber, sold ice cream and fish and owned a bakery and a cleaning and dyeing shop on the corner of Main and Fairchild Streets. In 1857, the governor nominated Noland notary public, but the secretary of state refused to allow the appointment because of Noland's race.[259]

Another of Madison's early black residents was Eston Hemings, the likely child of Thomas Jefferson and his slave Sally Hemings. Freed by Jefferson's will in 1829, Hemings moved to Madison in 1852 with his wife and three children. A cabinetmaker and musician, Hemings added Jefferson to his name when he moved to Wisconsin and passed as white, with his reddish hair and gray eyes, to allow his family more opportunities in their new home. Although he died of smallpox only four years after arriving in the city, his sons became successful Madison businessmen, and his widow lived at 121 North Webster Street for thirty-three more years.[260] Eston's eldest child, John W. Jefferson, was proprietor in the late 1850s of Madison's American House hotel across the street from the capitol. The middle child, Anna, married in Madison but died young. The youngest son, Beverley Jefferson, worked for his brother and served briefly in the Civil War before becoming proprietor of the American House himself. The whole family is buried in Forest Hill Cemetery.[261]

Madison's black population remained small until the twentieth century. Employment opportunities were limited, and most factories were segregated until thc start of World War II. Wisconsin, unlike its neighboring states, did not experience the sizable African American migration between the world wars, primarily because the state's agricultural and skilled manufacturing jobs did not offer many opportunities for African Americans. Most farms had single owner-operators who had little need for hired labor. Likewise, most unskilled factory jobs had already been taken by earlier immigrants. Scarcely concealed prejudice also discouraged black settlement.

Like other groups welcomed with less-than-open arms, Madison's black population started its own community organizations. The Free African Methodist Church, founded in 1902, was for many years the center of the city's small black community. A second black church, Mount Zion Baptist, opened in 1913. These and other social organizations provided direction and comfort to the city's blacks, especially important as white anxiety about black settlement remained high.[262]

Although Madison got a chapter of the National Association for the Advancement of Colored People (NAACP) in the 1920s, the organization struggled in its first years, lapsing for a decade before reorganizing in 1943. Leadership in the organization came from Madison's small black professional and business class. In its early years, the local chapter focused primarily on supporting national NAACP programs rather than tackling local social and economic problems. That began to change after World War II.

Employed African Americans were especially hard hit by the Depression. As late as March 1940, 46 percent of Wisconsin's black population was unemployed, compared to 13 percent for whites. The situation was only slightly better in Madison, where 25 percent remained without jobs.[263] Because most worked in largely unskilled jobs, African Americans in these positions were the first to go when businesses found themselves in trouble.

Discrimination certainly played a role in the high unemployment rate as well. A 1943 survey of Madison's employment policies revealed that department stores and utilities would only hire blacks for positions as maids and porters. Many heavy industries would not hire them at all. Only a packinghouse, railroad yard and two light industries reported regularly employing African Americans.[264]

By 1940, Wisconsin's African American population was extraordinarily concentrated in urban areas, mostly in Milwaukee, but a growing number in Madison. Compared to other Wisconsin cities, Madison was considered among the most congenial and welcoming in the state. Blacks could shop in nearly any store and could even own their own businesses. Even so, zoning codes kept blacks confined to three small areas of the city, all located to the east and south of the capitol, in largely substandard housing near railroad tracks, foundries and factories.[265]

World War II temporarily improved the economic prospects of Madison's black community. Labor shortages in critical wartime industries created opportunities that had previously been closed to blacks. Discrimination remained prevalent, though, and some jobs remained closed to blacks despite federal regulations and a presidential order prohibiting discrimination.

Many black residents served in the armed forces. At a time when most United Service Organizations (USOs) were segregated, Madison boasted two integrated facilities, one located downtown and the other at the First Unitarian Church. Dances remained segregated, however; busloads of black women came from Milwaukee and other southeast Wisconsin cities to take part.[266]

Only gradually and tentatively did civil rights make progress in Madison after World War II. As more African Americans came seeking jobs, race became the overriding factor that determined the circumstances under which they were allowed to settle and become part of the Madison community. Encountering discrimination in housing, employment and education, African Americans began to organize in greater numbers to remedy these injustices.

The civil rights movement developed more slowly among Wisconsin's blacks than among those in other states, despite some support for the movement among students at the University of Wisconsin. The number of African Americans in Madison was so small—with a population a little over fourteen hundred in 1960, whites outnumbered blacks eighty-three to one—that many residents concluded that Madison had no race problem.[267] Black and white families lived together in mixed neighborhoods, and their children attended the same schools. More than half owned their own homes. Restaurants, theaters, hotels, taxis and buses did not discriminate against African Americans, at least not openly, and seated blacks and whites beside one another. The police received instructions to treat blacks fairly, and hospitals provided the same treatment to blacks and whites. In 1954, the mayor had even created a Commission on Human Rights to improve race relations in the city.[268] The president of the Madison NAACP openly discouraged demonstrations, saying that they would not serve the same purpose as they did in places like Birmingham, Alabama. At least "not now," he added.[269] Many among Wisconsin's black community hoped that studies and surveys, rather than protests, might lead to a better understanding of the problems and the corrective steps needed.[270]

Below the surface, however, conditions were not nearly as rosy as many white residents wanted to believe. In employment and housing, in particular, opportunities for blacks remained far more limited than for whites. Lacking a heavily industrial base, Madison did not have the prospects for unskilled and semiskilled workers that existed in Milwaukee and other southeast Wisconsin cities. Many jobs in Madison required education and technical training that a lot of African Americans did not have, and most jobs did not offer on-the-job training. Many black adults had gone to school at a time when skilled jobs were unavailable to them, so they had had little incentive to acquire these skills. Others had been turned away despite their qualifications and were not aware that Madison employers had changed their hiring practices.[271]

Despite claims to the contrary, discrimination remained deeply ingrained in many hiring policies. Very few companies admitted that they would not hire African Americans. More often they simply told black applicants that no positions were available. Some were willing to offer blacks jobs but then actively discouraged them from actually taking the proffered job. Whether openly discriminatory or not, no Madison company actively sought out black employees, leading the state industrial commission to conclude in 1963 that Madison employers were simply perpetuating the status quo rather than increasing opportunities for all people, black and white.[272]

For Madison's African American community, this meant that most were still working unskilled jobs. Roughly half of black women worked in service jobs, primarily as maids, cooks and housecleaners. Only 10 percent of

Madison's black men and women held skilled jobs in industry, craft trades or clerical positions. African Americans also tended to earn less than their white counterparts, nearly one-third less than other working families. Blacks made the largest employment gains in government jobs in the late 1950s and early 1960s, although the overall number remained quite small compared to whites.[273] Velma Hamilton became Madison's first black teacher when she became an English professor at the Madison Area Technical College.

Besides employment, discriminatory housing practices plagued Madison. An NAACP survey in the late 1950s showed that three-fourths of Madison's black households were located in only two areas of Madison. Things had scarcely improved by 1960, when nearly 60 percent of the city's black residents lived in Greenbush or in South Madison.

The old and often run-down housing and commercial buildings in the Greenbush neighborhood housed a diverse mix of Italians, Jews, blacks and other ethnic groups. The neighborhood had fallen out of official favor during Prohibition, when it became a center of bootlegging, and the city's opinion had scarcely changed in the intervening years.[274] In the 1950s and 1960s, the city used federal urban renewal funds to purchase all of what it classified as "blighted" property. Between 1962 and 1964, whole blocks were bulldozed, and the neighborhood's residents were forced to find other housing, action that proved difficult, as many apartment owners would not even allow nonwhites to look at their property.

Many displaced blacks moved to Madison's south side, which became 60 to 70 percent black in some sections. South Madison was one of the few areas of the city where blacks could afford to build new homes. It was also the only place in the city where blacks could buy homes without hassle. Others found housing on the east side in subsidized housing by Truax Field and on the north side.

Like Greenbush, South Madison was targeted by the city for rehabilitation in the 1960s. Rather than tearing down all the buildings, the Madison Redevelopment Authority demolished some of the buildings and replaced them with similarly priced housing. This avoided the relocation problem that plagued the renewal of Greenbush. The city also put in sewers, streets, sidewalks, streetlights and parks.[275]

Discriminatory housing practices created obstacles for blacks of all social classes, however. Professional and middle-class blacks could often not break into all-white neighborhoods because white residents feared their property values would decline as a result. In 1962, for example, a black army officer could not find a space for his house trailer in Madison, despite vacancies in several trailer courts.[276]

Discrimination in private housing faced the strongest resistance, and bills prohibiting discrimination were widely opposed in the 1950s and early 1960s. A significantly watered-down version was eventually approved, but by exempting all owner-occupied, single-family homes and all owner-occupied rooming houses with fewer than five boarders, it effectively created a loophole for most Madison housing. In 1965, the state legislature approved a weak open-housing law. It was strengthened two years later, and Madison became one of the first cities in the state to approve open housing and to create its own nondiscriminatory housing ordinances.[277]

In 1969, Madison got its first black alderman, Eugene Parks. One of the city's most outspoken civil rights leaders, Parks began criticizing Madison's racial injustices as a high school student. He later served as Madison's first affirmative action director, but his criticisms of how the Madison Area Technical College handled its hiring of a new president led Mayor Joe Sensenbrenner to fire him for alleged incompetence in 1988. Parks claimed the firing was illegal and filed suit against the city. He won his case and was reinstated as a city employee. Parks ran for mayor in 1988 and 1999, making it all the way to the general election in 1999, the farthest a black candidate had ever advanced in a Madison mayoral race.[278]

Though imperfect, by the 1970s, the housing and employment situation for Madison's black community was improving. Blacks remained disproportionately clustered in certain areas of the city, a trend that continues to this day. They also continued to work lower-paying jobs.

School integration became a prominent issue in Madison in the 1980s. Madison's student population began to drop dramatically in the 1970s, forcing the closure of several schools, including Longfellow Elementary in Greenbush. The students were sent to Franklin Elementary and Lincoln Middle School, which reopened as an elementary school to accommodate the new students. Soon, the minority enrollment at both schools neared 50 percent, well above the district average of 16 percent. Several residents filed complaints with the federal Office for Civil Rights alleging intentional segregation. As a result, paired schools were created combining attendance areas of a largely white school with two minority ones.

The school plan changed the idea of neighborhood schools, mixing black and white schoolchildren to a significant degree for the first time in Madison's history. Opponents of the plan predicted massive white flight and declining property values, but neither happened. The concept was implemented with no violence or public protest. The paired schools, Franklin-Randall and Midvale-Lincoln, remain paired today.[279]

As the 1970s progressed, the nation's attention shifted from civil rights to other issues, such as the continuing war in Vietnam and the environment. Inspired by the civil rights movement, other social groups also began to assert their rights and demand equal protection. The 1969 Stonewall riots in New York helped transform the gay rights movement from small, localized activism into a widespread protest for equal rights and acceptance, particularly in the areas of housing and employment.

In 1982, Wisconsin became the first state in the country to outlaw discrimination based on sexual orientation. Tammy Baldwin of Madison became the first woman elected to Congress from Wisconsin and the first openly gay nonincumbent elected to the U.S. House of Representatives in 1998. Despite these notable firsts in gay rights, however, Wisconsin voters approved a constitutional amendment defining marriage as between one man and one woman in 2006, though the majority of Madison voters disapproved.

18

VIETNAM AND OPPOSITION AT HOME

In the mid-1960s, the energy of the civil rights movement merged with antiwar activism as American involvement in Vietnam escalated. Many of the students leading the war protests got their first taste of activism helping southern blacks with desegregation efforts and voter registration earlier in the decade. They now turned their attention and energy to stopping the longest and one of the most costly wars in U.S. history.

More than 58,000 Americans died and more than 300,000 were wounded in a war fought primarily in Vietnam from 1959 to 1975. The United States entered the war incrementally between 1950 and 1965, when President Lyndon Johnson began aggressively bombing North Vietnam and sent U.S. Marines to defend South Vietnam. The United States became involved in the war for a number of reasons, many of which evolved over time but had largely to do with containing communism. Increased U.S. involvement was matched by a rise of antiwar protest in the 1960s, as dissenting groups formed at many of the nation's universities, including the campuses of the University of Wisconsin. In the early 1960s, however, the majority of Americans supported the Johnson administration's claim that it was fighting to stop communism in Southeast Asia, as the United States had done in Korea a decade before, and were unaware that this gradually escalating war would forever alter American society.

The war pitted the North Vietnamese and the National Liberation Front (NLF, or Vietcong) against the United States and the South Vietnamese army. From 1946 until 1954, a unified Vietnamese population had fought for its independence from France. At the end of that struggle, the country had been temporarily divided into two governing units.

As the two governments continually fought against each other after 1954, the United States began to supply more and more aid and soldiers to South Vietnam. In 1965, when it appeared that North Vietnam might win, the United States sent large numbers of troops to prevent South Vietnam from collapsing. By 1969, more than 500,000 U.S. soldiers were stationed in Vietnam, and another 1.2 million were positioned elsewhere in Southeast Asia. Although Congress never officially declared war, the conflict in Vietnam took the lives of many thousands of soldiers and inflicted huge social, political and economic costs on the nation.

Opinion of the war was mixed, even amongst those fighting. Writing to his professor at the University of Wisconsin, student-soldier Benjamin Morgan noted, "This is a war begun strictly by political elements in the American Congress…Vietnam has not been worth the price. War has never been productive, and our investment here will reap very little return." Veterans who felt similarly to Morgan organized the Madison Veterans for Peace in Vietnam in 1967 to challenge the notion that dissent indicated a lack of patriotism, particularly among former soldiers. Other Madison residents were more enthusiastic, or at least more willing to trust the motives of the American government.

At home, many Madison residents supported the Vietnam War at first, but as the Johnson administration increased U.S. involvement, dissatisfaction turned into organized protest. Early protests centered on the morality of U.S. military involvement. Antiwar sentiment increased following the Tet Offensive of 1968, and after Johnson's successor, President Richard Nixon, escalated U.S. involvement. As more Americans died, protests grew rapidly. Soon, virtually no college or university in the United States was without an organized student movement, often led by the left-wing Students for a Democratic Society (SDS) or allied groups, with Madison at the forefront.

The Madison campus of the University of Wisconsin gained a reputation as one of the nation's most radical campuses in the 1960s as antiwar demonstrations mobilized thousands of students. Most of the students had come to UW to learn and have fun, not to protest. But as the war escalated, more students were drawn into activist roles.

One of those students was Paul Soglin, who later became mayor of Madison. Soglin came from a family of activists in Chicago. He entered the University of Wisconsin in 1962, chosen in part for its minimal ROTC requirement for students. Once on campus, Soglin eagerly joined the protest culture, serving as secretary of the local branch of the Student Nonviolent Coordinating Committee, the local branch of a major civil rights organization. He also participated in the first major campus demonstration, a protest against American support for Ngo Dinh Diem, the repressive president of South Vietnam.

Students were not the only ones leading protests. Some early antiwar events were organized by faculty, including an April 1, 1965 teach-in, only the second such event in the nation, led by future UW chancellor William Sewell. Teach-ins provided discussion forums for students and faculty on war issues.

Demonstrations increased after the Selective Service changed its draft policy. Although thousands of students received student deferments from the draft, they still lived at the mercy of the Selective Service. A 1966 policy change that increased the chances of those with poor grades being drafted led to one of Madison's largest demonstrations to date. Soglin joined the first sit-in at an administration building; it lasted several days and resulted in the university administration agreeing to review its draft policy. Other students marched, burned draft cards and confronted army recruiters.

Tensions came to a head in October 1967, when students protesting the makers of the weapon napalm, Dow Chemical, which was recruiting employees on campus, turned violent. This was not the first Dow-related protest on campus. Students had staged a sit-in earlier in the year in February that had remained peaceful. Dow's return trip in October was a different story. More than one thousand students gathered outside the building where Dow interviews were taking place, while Soglin and others blocked an inside hallway. The Madison police, called to the scene by Chancellor Sewell, arrived wearing helmets and carrying nightsticks. No one had ever called the city police to campus before. Unable to broker a compromise with the students, the chancellor ordered the police to clear out the protestors; they did so with a brutal force unseen before on campus. The police beat students on their heads, backs and stomachs with their clubs and used tear gas to drive them away. Dozens, including Soglin, were injured. Forty-seven students were taken to the hospital.

University of Wisconsin students clash with riot police during a demonstration against Dow Chemical's involvement in Vietnam in 1967. *Wisconsin Historical Society Image ID #2289.*

The police violence helped to radicalize many formerly apolitical students. It also marked the first time that a campus antiwar demonstration had turned violent, an event that would have long-lasting effects.

Soglin, betrayed by the violent response to what he felt was a peaceful protest, decided to try a new approach and began looking for ways to work for change from within the political system. One year later, in April 1968, Soglin was elected town alderman for Madison's Eighth District. In 1973, the same year a cease-fire agreement was reached in Paris, he became the mayor.[280]

The Mifflin Street Block Party began in 1969 in the heat of the Vietnam War. At the center of the city's antiwar protests, the Mifflin neighborhood decided to hold a celebration of the community being created around grassroots antiwar activism. But what began as a party ended in three days of violence as the police attempted to clear the partiers from the streets. The police used tear gas and billy clubs to disperse the crowds and were met with thrown rocks, bricks and bottles, as well as various student-constructed barricades. The event continued on after the war, though it lost much of its focus on political protest and became, instead, a general spring celebration for students.

Another disturbing event took place on campus on August 24, 1970. Early that morning, four young men, members of the antiwar group the New Year's Gang, parked a stolen Ford Econoline van filled with close to two thousand pounds of ammonium nitrate topped with fuel oil next to Sterling Hall. The building was home to the Army Mathematics Research Center, an army-funded think tank that helped create new weapons. At 3:42 a.m., shortly after they lit the fuse, the bomb exploded, destroying a large portion of the building, injuring four men inside and killing Robert Fassnacht, a promising young physicist.

The group had not intended to hurt, much less kill, anyone. They had thought that if they bombed a building on a Monday morning when school was not in session, and if they notified the police beforehand, no one would be harmed. Unfortunately, things did not go as planned. After learning of Fassnacht's death, the four fled Madison. Three of the four were eventually caught and jailed.[281]

While many feared that the bombing would escalate tensions and encourage more violent protests, Sterling Hall brought a sudden halt to the violence. A calmer mood spread—one that discouraged violence in the name of peace. Until the Oklahoma City bombing of 1995, Sterling Hall remained the largest act of domestic sabotage.

Ultimately, the United States failed to achieve its goal of propping up the government of South Vietnam as the North Vietnamese and Vietcong forces managed to occupy more and more territory in the south. Their successes, combined with growing voter disenchantment with the war in the United States, prompted the government to start peace negotiations, which were signed in January 1973. U.S. troops were withdrawn two months later. The end of hostilities finally came in April 1975, when the southern capital of Saigon (now called Ho Chi Minh City) fell to Communist forces and Vietnam reunified under Communist control as the Socialist Republic of Vietnam.

19

GREENING MADISON

Our goal is not just an environment of clean air and water and scenic beauty. The objective is an environment of decency, quality and mutual respect for all other human beings and all living creatures." So proclaimed Wisconsin senator Gaylord Nelson on the nation's first Earth Day, April 22, 1970.

When Earth Day began in 1970, few people expected it to become a globally observed holiday. But the idea that began in Wisconsin has become a world event, celebrated by more than a billion people in 190 countries. Earth Day was not Wisconsin's first contribution to environmental awareness, however.

Concern for the environment emerged as a complex and broadly popular movement in the United States in the late nineteenth century. Newly urbanized Americans were becoming increasingly aware of the importance of nature as an economic, aesthetic and spiritual resource, leading to unprecedented public and private initiatives to ensure the conservation of natural resources and the preservation of wildlife and land. This impulse drove the Madison Park and Pleasure Drive Association to set aside green space and create Madison's first parks in the early twentieth century. At the same time, Wisconsin—and Madison because of the university—had become a center of conservation thinking and activity.

Increase Lapham (the same person who first systematically investigated Indian mounds all over the state, including in the Madison area) is generally considered the founder of the conservation movement in Wisconsin. Arriving in Milwaukee three days before Wisconsin became a territory in 1836, Lapham kept careful records on the environment that served as models for those who followed him.

In the 1850s, Lapham began to argue for an ecological point of view toward the Wisconsin frontier. In 1855, he urged the state legislature to authorize a natural history survey before any more of Wisconsin's native species became extinct under the brunt of white settlement and industrialization. He also warned about the devastation of state forests, fifty years before it became an issue of national importance. Lapham's book, *Report on the Disastrous Effects of the Destruction of Forest Trees, Now Going on So Rapidly in the State of Wisconsin*, published in 1867, was one of the first to stress the importance of natural resources. He wrote other books about the state's native grasses and Indian effigy mounds and was a charter member of the State Historical Society of Wisconsin in Madison.

That same decade, Wisconsin's—and perhaps the nation's—best-known environmental thinker was immersed in farm chores near Portage. Though he would achieve his greatest fame for his years in California, John Muir spent his formative years on a farm in Wisconsin. In 1849, the Muir family immigrated to the United States from Scotland. Until he entered the University of Wisconsin in 1861, Muir worked on his family farm near Portage, roaming the fields and woods whenever he had the chance. Muir was also an inventor, creating an alarm clock that would tip up his bed and dump him on the floor, as well as a desk that rotated his schoolbooks after a preset time studying. He showed this "early-rising machine" at the 1860 Wisconsin State Fair in Madison. Muir later wrote that his strenuous years in Wisconsin's outdoors prepared him for his later wilderness ramblings.

Robert La Follette's Progressive politics influenced the rise of conservation concerns on the state level in the early twentieth century. La Follette worked closely with university professors, including geologist and university president Charles Van Hise, on ways to protect Wisconsin's natural resources from complete economic exploitation. Van Hise chaired the State Conservation Commission, wrote the first conservation textbook in 1910 and even provided council to President Teddy Roosevelt.

The creation of state-owned and protected parks was a major Progressive-era conservation measure. In 1907, the state legislature created a State Park Board. It hired John Nolen, who was already at work on Madison's city plan, to draft a feasibility report for a State Park System. These early conservation efforts would inspire later generations of environmentalists, who would introduce new goals to the movement.

While the conservation movement had viewed natural resources as commodities to produce material goods, the emerging environmental movement grew out of an interest in outdoor recreation. Rather than using resources efficiently, environmentalists sought to protect natural resources from use for aesthetic, moral or spiritual reasons.

Aldo Leopold became one of the most notable figures of the early environmental movement. He inspired people to appreciate wildlife and to use the land sensibly and sensitively. Born in Iowa in 1887, Leopold developed many of his insights while spending time at his family cabin, known as the "shack," near Baraboo. He carefully observed and recorded every detail of the plants and animals around him, recognizing how everything in nature was connected. Out of this observation came his most famous book, *A Sand County Almanac*, published in 1949, one year after his death.

Leopold came to Madison in 1924 to serve as associate director of the Forest Products Laboratory. He also began teaching at the University of Wisconsin. His continued investigation of the practice and philosophy of conservation led to the publication of the first textbook in the field of wildlife management, *Game Management*, in 1933. Later that year, Leopold became chair of the nation's first Game Management department at UW, a new field that combined forestry, agriculture, biology, zoology, ecology, education and communication to manage and restore wildlife populations.

Leopold also oversaw research at the new University of Wisconsin Arboretum. Speaking at the 1934 dedication, Leopold mused:

> *Perhaps we should not call the place an arboretum at all…Our idea…is to reconstruct primarily for the use of the university, a sample of original Wisconsin—a sample of what Dane County looked like when our ancestors arrived here in the 1840s…before we took it away from the Indians.*[282]

His words reflected the change in the movement from the earlier conscious use of nature to the protection and restoration rhetoric of the emerging environmental movement.

Serving on the Wisconsin Conservation Commission in the 1940s, Leopold helped to formulate policies that emphasized the management of land not just for commercial uses but also for the benefit of humans, animals and plants. Leopold's work helped give rise to a new attitude toward wildlife as an object of observation rather than of sport hunting.

This new perspective on animals and natural resources that developed in the 1940s and 1950s ultimately led to the federal endangered species act, state-sponsored wildlife programs, a heightened interest in plant and animal habitats and a new focus on biological diversity. University of Wisconsin professors played an increasingly larger role in state natural resource policymaking as well, advising on everything from science to administration and enforcement.

The environmental movement's emphasis on the preservation of specific resources in a more natural environment led to the creation of the National Wilderness Preservation System in 1964, the National Trails System in 1968 and a public purchase program in the Land and Water Conservation Act of 1964.

In the 1960s, Wisconsin governor Gaylord Nelson established a national reputation as a leader in environmental protection with his advocacy of Wisconsin's pioneering Outdoor Recreation Act. Passed in 1961, the act pledged $50 million toward environmental planning, land acquisition and state highway easements. The program ended up protecting fifty-four thousand acres of land in Wisconsin by collecting a one-cent-per-pack tax on cigarettes.

Elected to the U.S. Senate in 1962, Nelson proposed a constitutional amendment stating that "every person has the inalienable right to a decent environment." Borrowing a tactic of the anti–Vietnam War protests, the teach-in, Nelson suggested a full day of teaching and learning about the environment in a 1969 speech in Seattle. Nelson believed that if people knew more about the environment, they would take better care of it and demand better protection. His efforts led to the first Earth Day on April 22, 1970.

Madison's Earth Day celebration was typical of other big university towns. Some observers gathered at Picnic Point at 4:45 a.m. for an "Earth Service," during which they read works by Aldo Leopold, Rachel Carson and Henry David Thoreau. The city and the UW devoted a whole week to the event, which included environmental art exhibits, a film festival, tours of the arboretum and dozens of workshops and talks on topics such as "Ecologically Sound Community Planning," "Population Growth and Society" and "Life or Death for the Oceans."[283] Meanwhile, Girl Scouts

A march on the first Earth Day in 1970. *Wisconsin Historical Society Image ID #48103.*

distributed pamphlets prepared by UW graduate students throughout the city advocating household action everyone could take to save the planet.[284]

In response to Nelson's efforts, Congress created a governmental agency, the Environmental Protection Agency (EPA), to repair existing environmental damage and to establish policies to keep the environment safe and clean. It also passed the Water Quality Improvement Act and the Air Quality Control Act to make clean water and air universally available.

At the same time that protecting natural resources became national concerns, interest in a parallel movement concerned with the preservation of cultural and historic resources was growing. The United States Congress passed the National Historic Preservation Act in 1966, giving the federal government a leading role in preserving archaeological sites and historic structures and objects. The act marked the culmination of efforts to protect the nation's historic sites and landscapes that began in the nineteenth century.

Among its many provisions, the act created the National Register of Historic Places and encouraged states to create their own State Historic Preservation Offices. Wisconsin's state office is located at the Wisconsin Historical Society in Madison. Thirty-four Madison properties are listed on the National Register, along with three national historic districts.

Locally, the Madison Landmarks Commission and the Common Council have designated more than 160 buildings and sites as Madison landmarks. The Landmarks Commission got its start in 1971 after a venerable historic home was torn down and replaced by a Burger King. Mayor William Dyke spearheaded the effort, which set out policies and procedures to designate historic buildings as local landmarks, a different procedure than a listing on the National Register, though some properties appear on both lists. The commission was charged with approving exterior alterations to landmarks and was given the authority to delay demolition of a historic building. In 1980, the Landmarks Commission gained the power to deny demolitions altogether.

Madison archaeologist and historian Charles E. Brown was a leader and innovator in historic preservation long before it existed as an academic discipline. Alarmed at the destruction of Indian mounds occurring throughout the state in the early 1900s, Brown urged the Wisconsin Archaeological Society, which he had founded and for which he served as editor and secretary, to make the preservation of the mounds a top priority. He helped them develop a plan to do so—involving surveys, protective legislation, public acquisition and stewardship, partnerships, fundraising, landmarking and relentless promotion and education—which formed the foundation of Wisconsin's first historic preservation movement. Brown personally surveyed the mounds and other ancient Indian sites in Madison himself. Working with the Landmarks Committee of the Federated Women's Clubs of Wisconsin, the Daughters of the American Revolution, local historical societies and other public service organizations, the Wisconsin Archaeological Society placed historic markers on mound groups across the state to call public attention to these important ancient structures. He also cultivated close relationships with the Ho-Chunk and other Indian communities to gather information on their beliefs, history and culture.

In 1911, a Wisconsin Archaeological Society delegation under Brown's leadership successfully lobbied the legislature to pass a state law to protect antiquities and archaeological sites on public lands—Wisconsin's first historic preservation law. A 1985 state law prohibiting the disturbance of burial sites on private and public lands came too late to protect most of the state's mounds from destruction. However, several hundred mounds in Madison have been protected, most designated as city landmarks, and the city has actively promoted their listing on the National Register of Historic Places.[285]

As the twentieth century progressed, archaeologists and historic preservationists became strong supporters of efforts to protect the environment through public and private land acquisition, recognizing that the creation of "natural areas" and conservation parks also offered protection to the archaeological and cultural sites contained within these landscapes. Madison's Conservation Parks Program began in 1971, after the city began purchasing land in what is now Cherokee Marsh to help protect and restore the landscape. The city currently manages more than sixteen hundred acres of conservation parkland, including Cherokee Marsh, Edna Taylor Conservation Park, Prairie Ridge Park and Turville Point.

Gaylord Nelson, too, made it explicitly clear that concern for the environment included the "built" environment as well. Run-down neighborhoods and decayed buildings became "blighted environments" that could be cleaned up, recycled and reused, creating historic neighborhoods out of existing infrastructure and revitalizing communities. These efforts were not always done with the most sensitivity, however, as hundreds of Greenbush residents found themselves without homes during the demolition of the area in the 1950s and 1960s. To encourage the reuse of older buildings, a tax credit program for the rehabilitation of historic structures was created in 1976; it has returned more than $1 billion to Wisconsin home and business owners since its inception.

Madison got its now-iconic Saturday farmers' market in 1972. Farmers had sold produce and other goods at markets on East Washington Avenue and at the City Market on Blount Street in the late nineteenth and early twentieth centuries. But for most of the twentieth century, Madison was without a good farmers' market. In 1972, Mayor Bill Dyke called on the Dane County Extension Office and the newly formed Central Madison Committee, whose mission was the revitalization of downtown Madison, to help him create an open-air farmers' market like those that existed in Europe. Together with the chamber of commerce, the idea for the Dane County Farmers' Market was born.

Area farmers had already found their own creative outlets for sale, however. Parking lots at grocery stores and malls, gas stations and busy street corners were popular places for farmers to sell produce directly to customers. Not every place welcomed farmers on site, though, as grower Jonathan Barry found out when he attempted to sell his vegetables in front of Ella's Deli on State Street in 1972. Looking for a reliable place for

The Dane County Farmers' Market is the nation's largest producer-only market, held every Saturday morning year round. *Erika Janik.*

farmers like himself to sell goods, Barry was soon hired to manage the new Dane County Farmers' Market.

With the mayor's support, the capitol grounds became home to the new market, which opened on September 30, 1972. Eager customers overwhelmed the eleven vendors who set up shop that first Saturday. One week later, eighty-five sellers greeted several thousand customers. By 1974, the market had become so popular that Barry began issuing season passes for the stalls in an effort to organize the vendors. The only rule then, and one still enforced today, was that all products be Wisconsin grown. Today, approximately three hundred vendors sell throughout the year.[286]

Wisconsin has long placed a priority on environmental health and safety. The voluntary Green Tier Law, for example, rewards environmental performance that goes beyond the minimum standards for air, water, land and natural resources required by law. Green Tier allows the state to distinguish between good environmental performers and those performing at or near the regulatory minimums and provides incentives for businesses to improve their existing environmental programs. In 2007, Wisconsin launched the statewide initiative Travel Green Wisconsin, the first ecotourism certification program in the nation, which recognizes travel-related businesses that have taken specific actions toward environmental, social and economic sustainability. Other programs, like the Wisconsin Environmental Education Board, provide Wisconsin citizens with additional ways to be involved in environmental education, leadership and reform.

In recent years, Madison has taken even more aggressive steps to green its future. Mayor Dave Cieslewicz developed a Green Capitol City Plan in 2004 to increase Madison's energy efficiency. In 2005, the city formally adopted a sustainability framework known as "The Natural Step" to guide and facilitate future environmental decisions. The framework encourages policymakers to weigh choices against a set of conditions that support both people and the environment. Among the projects the city has undertaken under the new program are reducing energy waste in city buildings, providing commuting incentives for car-free travel and using green cleaning supplies and services. The city has also invested in alternative transportation options, such as bicycle paths (including the seven miles of the Capitol City Trail that pass through the city) and hybrid city buses.

Madison's environmental achievements have earned the city a raft of accolades. In 2000, the Environmental News Network recognized Madison as one of the nation's most environmentally friendly cities. The city has also been recognized as having some of the best walking and biking in the country, as well as the nation's best farmers' market.

Conclusion

INTO THE FUTURE

Over the years, Madison has developed a civic personality that is vital but not restless, sophisticated and friendly. Few people who have lived in Madison ever move away of their own free will." In its September 6, 1948 issue, *Life* magazine proclaimed Madison the best city in America. Residents paged through photos showing their city's peaceful parks, gracious homes and beautiful lakes in a piece titled "The Good Life in Madison." And for many in Madison, life was pretty good.

The *Life* article became the first of many to praise Madison, seemingly fulfilling the promise that John Nolen had seen forty years before in his seminal 1911 plan for the city. While few residents had been ready to embrace Nolen's vision of Madison at the time, by the mid- to late twentieth century, the praise seemed to many residents to be well deserved. Madison had finally become a model city as Nolen had predicted. It was only the first of what became a torrent of praise.

In 1996, *Money* magazine rated Madison America's best city, and it has continued to make *Money*'s list of one hundred best places to live nearly every year since. Madison has also been hailed as one of the best places to raise a family, to educate a child, to walk, to bike, to start a business (especially a technology-related one), to retire, to enjoy the arts, to be a vegetarian, to read, to grow old, to be outdoors, to be inspired and to find friendly people. The city that James Doty, Simeon Mills, the Pecks, Leonard Farwell and so many other early residents and promoters struggled to build has finally come into its own.

Coming out of the Vietnam War and into the last decades of the twentieth century, Madison city politics was largely dominated by liberal and Progressive politics. Paul Soglin, who was so active in Vietnam protests, served as mayor twice, from 1973 to 1979 and from 1989 to 1997. Soglin's election represented a shift in Madison's political culture away from conservative leaders and the violence that marked the Vietnam years. His election was also emblematic of many activists who transformed themselves into government officials and administrators in the 1970s and 1980s and tended to emphasize good government and class-bridging coalitions. Soglin, like other Progressive city mayors around the country in the 1970s, created a foreign policy for Madison independent of the rest of the country. As such, Soglin became the first U.S. mayor to visit Cuban leader Fidel Castro in 1975, a trip of great symbolic importance to Madison. The city has continued to take stands on foreign affairs, including a 2002 Madison Common Council proclamation opposing war in Iraq.

Adding to the political field, a new local political party, Progressive Dane, was founded in 1992 with a primary focus on city and county issues. Party members serve on the city council, the Dane County Board of Supervisors and the Madison School Board.

State government and the University of Wisconsin continued to dominate the city's economy. However, in the 1980s and early 1990s, the city experienced significant growth in the health, technology, advertising and insurance sectors. The University of Wisconsin has actively fostered the development of high-tech companies, especially in biotech, by working with local businesses and entrepreneurs to transfer academic research into real-world settings. Epic Systems Corporation, founded in 1979 in Madison to create electronic health records, is Dane County's most powerful business, employing more than three thousand people. Madison is also home to one of the world's largest online clothing retailers, Shopbop.

Concern about the loss of farmland to development in the 1960s spurred the creation of land-use plans and the establishment of a Regional Planning Commission in recent decades. To control sprawl, officials began talking about moratoriums on rural development in the 1970s, a concept that persisted with little actual effect into the 1990s. Many farmers wanted to keep the option of selling their land to developers and opposed any plan that set boundaries on development. The focus on controlling rural development did not include the city's land annexations, however, as

Madison's land area grew by 299 percent between 1950 and 1990. Just as Madison's boundaries began expanding across the beltline highway circling the city, Dane County began buying up many of the area's most precious natural areas to preserve them.

Madison has also gained new public spaces. Monona Terrace Community and Convention Center opened on the shores of Lake Monona in 1997, fifty-nine years after Frank Lloyd Wright first proposed the plan in 1938. Wright's original plan for the site included offices, courtrooms, a seven-thousand-seat auditorium, a railroad station, a parking ramp, a boat marina and a huge rooftop garden. Using the capitol as a model, he gave the building a circular shape, a domed fountain and roofline equal to the height of Wilson Street so as to not block the view of the capitol. Wright failed to sell his original plan to the city, but in 1953, city leaders convinced him to submit his plan again. Wright worked on the plan until his death in 1959, but the plan faltered again and was tabled for decades. At the urging of Mayor Paul Soglin, Monona Terrace was revived in the early 1990s, and funding was secured through public and private sources. Nearly sixty years after its conception, Monona Terrace finally opened in 1997.

The Frank Lloyd Wright–designed Monona Terrace. *Erika Janik.*

One year later, in 1998, philanthropist W. Jerome Frautschi made the first of what would become one of the world's largest donations to the arts: a $50 million donation to the city for a performing arts complex. By the time the Overture Center opened its doors in 2004, Frautschi had donated more than $200 million to its construction. The venue plays host to symphonies, operas, musicals, lectures and rock concerts.

Madison continues to grow and change at a feverish pace. The city and surrounding Dane County are the fastest-growing areas in the state. It's hard to imagine that Madison ever had a problem attracting residents or that the city's most iconic building, the capitol, might have easily been located in another city.

Madison's history is still being written, incorporating the lives and experiences of all who call Madison home. As the city looks to the future, Madison must continue to balance its zest for change and innovation with a healthy respect for its history and tradition, remembering that what we all hold dear will provide a way forward for all Madison residents.

NOTES

CHAPTER 1

1. Mollenhoff, *Madison*, 4.
2. Ibid., 7.
3. Ibid., 11.

CHAPTER 2

4. Durrie, *History of Madison*, 13.
5. Knapp, "Early Reminiscences," 380, 383.
6. Childs, "Recollections," 187–91.
7. Ibid.
8. Mollenhoff, *Madison*, 18.
9. Ibid., 20.

CHAPTER 3

10. *Dictionary of Wisconsin History*, s.v. "James Duane Doty," Wisconsin Historical Society, www.wisconsinhistory.org/topics/doty.

11. Odd Wisconsin, "How Madison Became the Capital," Wisconsin Historical Society, www.wisconsinhistory.org/odd/archives/002065.asp.
12. John V. Suydam in Draper, "Naming of Madison," 392.
13. Mollenhoff, *Madison*, 24.
14. Odd Wisconsin, "How Madison Became the Capital."
15. Mollenhoff, *Madison*, 25.

Chapter 4

16. Peck, "Reminiscenccs," 348.
17. Ibid., 350.
18. *Madison Democrat*, "First White Child Born in Madison," September 23, 1917.
19. Childs, "Recollections," 187–91.
20. Ruth Bradish, "Pigs in State Capitol Once Made Legislature Adjourn," *Wisconsin State Journal*, August 13, 1922.
21. Mollenhoff, *Madison*, 34.
22. Ibid., 35.
23. Durrie, *History of Madison*, 162.
24. Mollenhoff, *Madison*, 37.
25. Simeon Mills quoted in Butterfield, *History of Dane County*, 681.
26. Curators' Favorites, "Arndt Vest," Wisconsin Historical Society, www.wisconsinhistory.org/museum/artifacts/archives/001055.asp.

Chapter 5

27. Mollenhoff, *Madison*, 44.
28. *Dictionary of Wisconsin History*, s.v. "Leonard James Farwell," Wisconsin Historical Society, www.wisconsinhistory.org/dictionary/index.asp?action=view&term_id=2491.
29. *Wisconsin Express*, February 26, 1850; Smith, "History of Madison," 22–23.
30. Mollenhoff, *Madison*, 46.
31. Levitan, *Madison*, 24.
32. Mollenhoff, *Madison*, 45.

33. Leuchter and Zellie, *Third Lake Ridge.*
34. *Wisconsin State Journal*, May 24, 1854.
35. Mollenhoff, *Madison*, 53.
36. Ibid., 53.

Chapter 6

37. *Wisconsin State Journal*, August 8, 1856.
38. *Argus and Democrat*, May 1, 1856.
39. *Daily Patriot*, November 26, 1856.
40. Mollenhoff, *Madison*, 75.
41. *Wisconsin State Journal*, November 19, 1857.
42. Mollenhoff, *Madison*, 78.
43. State of Wisconsin, *Private and Local Laws*, 10–14.
44. Youngerman, "Theater Buildings," 283–84.
45. Current, *Civil War Era*, 221.
46. *Wisconsin State Journal*, January 10, 1861.
47. Ibid., April 19, 1861.
48. Ibid., April 27, 1861.
49. Ibid., March 7, 1864.
50. Mollenhoff, *Madison*, 95.
51. Hurn, *Wisconsin Women*, 42–45.
52. Hibbard, "History of Agriculture," 123.
53. Merk, *Economic History*, 208.
54. Smith, "History of Madison," 30.
55. Common Council Proceedings, April 28, 1865, Madison, WI.
56. Levitan, *Madison*, 50.
57. *Wisconsin State Journal*, September 1, 1865.

Chapter 7

58. Albert G. Tuttle, "Letter Written from Fort Winnebago in 1847," *Baraboo Republic*, May 25, 1922. Available online at www.wisconsinhistory.org/turningpoints/search.asp?id=805.
59. Mollenhoff, *Madison*, 63.

60. Ohio History Central, "Know-Nothing Party," Ohio Historical Society, www.ohiohistorycentral.org/entry.php?rec=911.
61. *Argus and Democrat*, May 28, 1853.
62. Mollenhoff, *Madison*, 67.
63. *Wisconsin State Journal*, March 4, 1870.
64. Mollenhoff, *Madison*, 142.
65. *Wisconsin State Journal*, September 14, 1866.
66. Ibid., February 11, 1886.
67. *Madison Democrat*, May 18, 1875.
68. *Wisconsin State Journal*, November 9, 1916.
69. Ibid., December 13, 1910.
70. Ibid., February 23, 1913; March 18, 1917.
71. Goldsmith, "German-Jewish and Russian-Jewish Immigration," 28–44.

Chapter 8

72. Mollenhoff, *Madison*, 113.
73. Rasmus Anderson, "Ole Bull, Norwegian Violinist, Appeared in Madison in 1868," *Wisconsin State Journal*, February 3, 1924.
74. Mollenhoff, *Madison*, 159–60.
75. Ibid., 160.
76. "Wisconsin Stories: Passing Through: Fuller Opera House," Wisconsin Public Television, www.wisconsinstories.com/2002season/passing/gallery/index.cfm.
77. *Wisconsin State Journal*, August 21, 1870; August 17, 1870.
78. Ibid., April 1, 1870.
79. Ordinance #22, June 19, 1856.
80. *Wisconsin State Journal*, June 27, 1879; Ordinance #772, July 15, 1879.
81. *Wisconsin State Journal*, December 9, 1899.
82. Mollenhoff, *Madison*, 235–36.
83. *Wisconsin State Journal*, December 2, 1913.
84. "WPR's Tradition of Innovation," Wisconsin Public Radio, www.wpr.org/about/hd_innovation.cfm.

CHAPTER 9

85. C.C. Britt quoted in Durrie, *History of Madison*, 142.
86. Butterfield, *History of Dane County*, 416–17.
87. *Fifty Years of Church Work*, 9–12.
88. Doane, *Grace Episcopal Church*, 11–17.
89. *Fifty Years of Church Work*, 14.
90. Mollenhoff, *Madison*, 145.
91. Durrie, *History of Madison*, 353.
92. *Wisconsin State Journal*, January 8, 1896; March 18, 1896.
93. Ibid., August 12, 1895.
94. Ibid., June 7, 1894; September 21, 1898.
95. Thwaites, *Historical Sketch*, 12–17.
96. Mollenhoff, *Madison*, 60.
97. Thwaites, *Historical Sketch*, 45–46.
98. *Wisconsin State Journal*, March 17, 1858.
99. Thwaites, *Historical Sketch*, 46.
100. Ibid.
101. Ruth Ann Montgomery, "Evansville Seminary," Evansville History, evansvillehistory.net/EvansvilleSeminary.html.
102. Mollenhoff, *Madison*, 140.
103. 1866 Board of Education Report, 7; 1870 Board of Education Report, 8–9.
104. Curti and Carstensen, *University of Wisconsin*, 501–607, 608.
105. Mollenhoff, *Madison*, 184.
106. Bob Kann, "All Their Ways are Helping Ways: Stories from the History of the Madison Public Library," Madison Public Library, www.madisonpubliclibrary.org/kann/index.
107. Atwood, "Dane County Press," 41.
108. Anderson, "Venturing into Politics."
109. Mollenhoff, *Madison*, 285.
110. Evjue, *Fighting Editor*, 121–70.
111. *Capital Times*, March 22, 1918.

Chapter 10

112. Suckow, *Madison City Directory*, 28; Jones, *Madison*, 160.
113. Common Council Proceedings, April 21, 1868.
114. *Wisconsin State Journal*, November 21, 1865; February 3, 1866; Suckow, *Madison City Directory*, 28–29.
115. *Wisconsin State Journal*, August 7, 1866.
116. Ibid., May 16, 1868.
117. Mollenhoff, *Madison*, 127.
118. *Wisconsin State Journal*, September 22, 1871.
119. Ibid., August 7, 1876.
120. Ibid., June 12, 1866.
121. Mollenhoff, *Madison*, 129.
122. *Wisconsin State Journal*, August 7, 1876; *Madison Democrat*, April 16, 1877.
123. Ibid., March 14, 1877.
124. Lawrence, "Wisconsin Ice Trade," 257–62.
125. *Wisconsin State Journal*, January 31, 1880; February 3, 9, 10, 23, 1880.
126. Mollenhoff, *Madison*, 163.
127. *Wisconsin State Journal*, November 29, 1881.
128. Larsen, *John A. Johnson.*
129. Ibid., 121–71.
130. Mollenhoff, *Madison*, 179.
131. *Madison Democrat*, September 26, 1899.
132. Flowers, *Annual Report*, xviii, xix.
133. *Wisconsin State Journal*, September 1, 1888.
134. Keyes, *History of Dane County*, 278; *Wisconsin State Journal*, January 7, 1885.
135. Sakrison, *Madison*, 64.
136. Mollenhoff, *Madison*, 167.
137. *Madison Points of Interest*, 2–3.

Chapter 11

138. *Wisconsin State Journal*, December 1, 1900.
139. Mollenhoff, *Madison*, 239.
140. *Wisconsin State Journal*, July 13, 1906.
141. Ibid., March 21, 1907.

142. Ibid., January 31, 1912.
143. Chapter 650, Laws of 1911.
144. Wisconsin State Legislature, Chapter 11, Special Session, 1912.
145. *Wisconsin State Journal*, March 14, 1914.
146. *Wisconsin State Journal*, August 11, 1906.
147. Mollenhoff, *Madison*, 292.
148. Wisconsin Historical Images, "Up in Smoke: The Story of the Capitol Fire of 1904," Wisconsin Historical Society, www.wisconsinhistory.org/whi/feature/smoke.
149. *Wisconsin State Journal*, July 25, 1903.
150. Ibid., June 25, 1903.
151. Ibid., September 1, 1901.
152. Levitan, *Madison*, 156.
153. *Wisconsin State Journal*, September 16, 1907.
154. Ibid., March 7, 1913; Mollenhoff, *Madison*, 302.
155. *Wisconsin State Journal*, December 19, 1916.
156. Evjue, *Fighting Editor*, 257–70.
157. *Wisconsin State Journal*, June 24, 1916; Chapter 453, Laws of 1915.
158. *Wisconsin State Journal*, June 30, 1917; June 28, 1917.
159. Ibid., March 25, 1904.
160. Ibid., February 11, 1903; May 13, 1903.
161. Ibid., October 24, 1905.
162. Mollenhoff, *Madison*, 299.
163. Ibid., 350.
164. *Madison Democrat*, November 3, 1900.
165. *Wisconsin State Journal*, December 31, 1916.
166. Hill, *Women in Gainful Occupations*, 286, 289.
167. Ibid., 229.

CHAPTER 12

168. Nolen, *Madison*, 16, 19, 139.
169. Mollenhoff, *Madison*, 218.
170. *Wisconsin State Journal*, February 27–28, 1893.
171. Ibid., April 17, 28, 1893.
172. http://www.lakeshorepreserve.wisc.edu/visit/mppda.htm.

173. Mollenhoff, *Madison*, 222.
174. Madison Park and Pleasure Drive Association, *Annual Report*, 1902, 58. Hereafter cited as MPPDA.
175. Ibid., 1899.
176. Ibid., 1923, 21–32, 58
177. Mollenhoff, *Madison*, 311.
178. Ibid., 315.
179. *Wisconsin State Journal*, December 7, 1910.
180. MPPDA, 1910, 1911, 1912.
181. Mollenhoff, *Madison*, 319.
182. MPPDA, 1912, 27–31; 1914, 20–21.
183. Ibid., 1908, 58.
184. Levitan, *Madison*, 172.
185. *Wisconsin State Journal*, March 30, 1908.
186. Ibid., April 28, 1908.
187. Ibid., December 9, 1908.
188. Ibid., December 6, 1908.
189. Mollenhoff, *Madison*, 329.
190. Common Council Proceedings, February 11, 1910; February 10, 1911.
191. *Wisconsin State Journal*, April 29, 1909.
192. Mollenhoff, *Madison*, 334.
193. Ibid., 334; Sachse, *Thousand Ages*.
194. Mollenhoff, *Madison*, 335.
195. *Wisconsin State Journal*, March 19, 1913.
196. Ibid., May 20, 21, 1916.
197. Ordinance #1520, January 31, 1910; Ordinance #1628, April 15, 1913.
198. Mollenhoff, *Madison*, 339.
199. *Wisconsin State Journal*, December 9, 1884.
200. Mollenhoff, *Madison*, 209.
201. *Wisconsin State Journal*, June 16, 1894.
202. Ibid., August 15, 1915.
203. Mollenhoff, *Madison*, 367.
204. *Wisconsin State Journal*, July 8, 1911.
205. Ibid., October 24, 1920.

Chapter 13

206. *Wisconsin State Journal*, August 5, 1914.
207. Ibid., November 20, 1914.
208. Mollenhoff, *Madison*, 386.
209. Levitan, *Madison*, 202.
210. *Capital Times*, February 13, 1918.
211. *Wisconsin State Journal*, September 26, 1917.
212. Ibid., April 27, 1917; January 13, 1918.
213. Ibid., June 12, 1917.
214. Cornbise, *War as Advertised.*
215. *Capital Times*, "Wisconsin in the First World War Faced Rationing Problems Just like Today's," December 13, 1943.
216. Women Students' War Work Council, *War Time Recipes*.
217. "Manual of Wheatless Recipes Issued by the Food Board of the Woman's Committee of the Dane County Council of Defense (1918)," Dane County Council of Defense Papers, Wisconsin Historical Society Archives, Madison, WI.
218. Janik, "Food Will Win," 25.
219. Mollenhoff, *Madison*, 388.
220. *Wisconsin State Journal*, September 18, 1917.
221. Larsen, *John A Johnson*, 202–03.
222. Mollenhoff, *Madison*, 388.
223. Glad, *History of Wisconsin*, 4–8.
224. Ibid., 58; *Milwaukee Journal*, October 19, 1918.
225. *Wisconsin State Journal*, December 10, 1918; "The Worst Flu Season in Wisconsin History," Wisconsin Historical Society, www.wisconsinhistory.org/highlights/archives/2006/01/the_worst_flu_s.asp.
226. *Wisconsin State Journal*, November 12, 1918.
227. Mollenhoff, *Madison*, 392.
228. Ibid., 392.

Chapter 14

229. *Wisconsin State Journal*, May 25, 1923; October 16, 1923; September 19, 1924.
230. Mollenhoff, "Capitol and Urban Planning," 38–49, 44.
231. United States Department of Labor, "Chapter 1: Start-up of the Department and World War I, 1913-1921," http://www.dol.gov/oasam/programs/history/dolchp01.htm.
232. Levitan, *Madison*, 208; Glad, *History of Wisconsin*, 123–24, 234.
233. Buckley, "Enforcement of Prohibition Laws," 1100–02; Glad, *History of Wisconsin*, 101–02.
234. Levitan, *Madison*, 186; "History," Neighborhood House Madison, www.neighborhoodhousemadison.org/history.
235. *Wisconsin State Journal*, June 10, 1919; Higham, *Strangers in the Land*, 259–61.
236. Glad, *History of Wisconsin*, 123.
237. *Capital Times*, March 20, 1930; August 13, 1930; December 17, 1930.
238. Ibid., March 1, 1930.
239. Levitan, *Madison*, 231.
240. *Capital Times*, March 6, 7, 1930; Glad, *History of Wisconsin*, 368–69.
241. *Wisconsin State Journal*, "Rebuilding Wisconsin: Work of New Deal–Era Programs Still Around Us," February 23, 2009.

Chapter 15

242. Thompson, *History of Wisconsin*, 96–97.
243. *Wisconsin State Journal*, January 12, 1945.
244. Thompson, *History of Wisconsin*, 79.
245. "History of MATC," Madison Area Technical College, http://matcmadison.edu/history-matc.
246. *Wisconsin State Journal*, January 12, 1945.
247. *International Directory*, s.v. "Madison-Kipp."
248. *Wisconsin State Journal*, December 4, 1944.
249. Thompson, *History of Wisconsin*, 100–01; Hartmann, *Home Front and Beyond*, 84–85, 90–95.
250. *Wisconsin State Journal*, September 24, 1944.

251. "The Impact of War Upon UW-Madison," Wisconsin Week, www.news.wisc.edu/wisweek/wartimeline.html.
252. *Wisconsin Blue Book*, 255–58.
253. "The Impact of War Upon UW-Madison," Wisconsin Week, www.news.wisc.edu/wisweek/wartimeline.html.

Chapter 16

254. Hemlin, "Wisconsin Korean War Stories," 25.
255. Mike Miller, "Downing a Demagogue," *Capital Times*, September 11, 2009; Thompson, *History of Wisconsin*, 443–601.
256. *Wisconsin State Journal*, "1951 Crusade for Freedom Opens in Madison This Week," November 11, 1951.
257. *Capital Times*, April 21, 1960.
258. "Living Under a Mushroom Cloud: Fear and Hope in the Atomic Age," Wisconsin Historical Museum Online Exhibit, www.wisconsinhistory.org/museum/atomic/takecovr.asp.

Chapter 17

259. Wisconsin State Journal, *Madison 150*, 25.
260. Ibid., 113.
261. Odd Wisconsin, "Thomas Jefferson's Madison Descendants?" Wisconsin Historical Society, www.wisconsinhistory.org/odd/archives/002089.asp.
262. *Wisconsin State Journal*, October 8, 1901; March 4, 1901; April 9, 1902.
263. Thompson, *History of Wisconsin*, 315.
264. Ibid., 317.
265. Ibid., 309.
266. *Milwaukee Journal*, November 12, 1967; *Capital Times*, March 31, 1943; April 9, 1943; Thompson, *History of Wisconsin*, 324.
267. *Eighteenth Census*, 65.
268. *Wisconsin State Journal*, "The Negro in Madison" series, July 28–August 25, 1963; NAACP, Madison Branch, "Negro Housing in Madison," 1959, 7–8, 24–25.
269. *Wisconsin State Journal*, July 30, 1963.

270. Thompson, *History of Wisconsin*, 340.
271. *Wisconsin State Journal*, August 13, 1963; Thompson, *History of Wisconsin*, 341; *Eighteenth Census*, 231, 434–37.
272. *Wisconsin State Journal*, August 11, 1963; findings of a November 21, 1963 hearing in Madison, in the hearing files, 1963–1966, Series 1747, Records of the Industrial Commission, Equal Opportunities Division, WSA; Thompson, *History of Wisconsin*, 342.
273. *Eighteenth Census*, 51, 65, 398–400; *Wisconsin State Journal*, August 11, 1963.
274. NAACP, "Negro Housing," 6–10, 24, 26; *Wisconsin State Journal*, August 4, 1963; Thompson, *History of Wisconsin*, 344.
275. Thompson, *History of Wisconsin*, 347; NAACP, "Negro Housing," 6–10.
276. NAACP, "Negro Housing," 11–16.
277. Thompson, *History of Wisconsin*, 392.
278. Wisconsin State Journal, *Madison 150*, 113; *Milwaukee Journal Sentinel*, "Madison Employee Gets New City Job after Firing," November 18, 1989.
279. Wisconsin State Journal, *Madison 150*, 72.

Chapter 18

280. "Two Days in October," *American Experience*, PBS, www.pbs.org/wgbh/amex/twodays/index.html.
281. Bates, *Rads*; Curators' Favorites, "Sterling Hall Bombing Engine Fragment," Wisconsin Historical Museum, www.wisconsinhistory.org/museum/artifacts/archives/001636.asp.

Chapter 19

282. Curt Meine, "Back to Nature at the UW Arboretum," *Isthmus*, May 29, 2009.
283. U.W. Organizations and Madison Civic Groups, "Earth Week."
284. "Gaylord Nelson and Earth Day: The Making of the Modern Environmental Movement," Wisconsin Historical Society, www.nelsonearthday.net.
285. "Charles E. Brown."
286. Carpenter and Carpenter, *Dane County Farmers' Market*, xi–xiv; "Market History," Dane County Farmers' Market on the Square, www.dcfm.org/history.asp.

BIBLIOGRAPHY

Anderson, Arlow W. "Venturing into Politics: The Norwegian American Press of the 1850's." *Wisconsin Magazine of History* 32 (1948–49).

Atwood, David. "The Dane County Press." *Proceedings of the Wisconsin Editorial Convention* (1865).

Bates, Tom. *Rads: The 1970 Bombing of the Army Mathematics Research Center of the University of Wisconsin and Its Aftermath.* New York: Harper Collins, 1992.

Birmingham, Bob, and Leslie Eisenberg. *Indian Mounds of Wisconsin.* Madison: University of Wisconsin Press, 2000.

Buckley, Frank. "Enforcement of the Prohibition Laws: Official Records of the National Commission on Law Observance and Enforcement: A Prohibition Survey of the State of Wisconsin." In *Enforcement of the Prohibition Laws, Official Records of the National Commission on Law Observance and Enforcement.* Vol. 4. Washington, D.C.: Government Printing Office, 1931.

Buenker, John D. *The History of Wisconsin.* Vol. 5, *War, A New Era, and Depression, 1914–1940.* Madison: State Historical Society of Wisconsin, n.d.

Butterfield, C.W. *History of Dane County, Wisconsin...Preceded by a History of Wisconsin, Statistics of the State, and an Abstract of Its Laws and Constitution and of the Constitution of the United States.* Chicago: Western Historical Company, 1880.

———. *History of the University of Wisconsin.* Madison: University Press Company, 1879.

Carpenter, Mary, and Quentin Carpenter. *The Dane County Farmers' Market: A Personal History*. Madison: University of Wisconsin Press, 2003.

"Charles E. Brown and the Indian Mounds of Madison." *Historic Madison: A Journal of the Four Lakes Region* 13 (1996).

Childs, Ebenezer. "Childs Recollections." *Wisconsin Historical Collections* 4 (1859).

Cornbise, Alfred. *War as Advertised: The Four Minute Men and America's Crusade, 1917–1918*. Philadelphia: American Philosophical Society, 1984.

Current, Richard N. *The History of Wisconsin*. Vol. 2, *The Civil War Era*. Madison: State Historical Society of Wisconsin, 1976.

Curti, Merle, and Vernon Carstensen. *The University of Wisconsin: 1848 to 1925, A History*. Vol. 1. Madison: University of Wisconsin Press, 1949.

Doane, Gilbert H. *Grace Episcopal Church: A History of the Parish Commemorating the Centennial Anniversary of the First Service Held in Grace Church*. Madison, WI: Democrat Printing Company, 1958.

Draper, L.C. "Naming of Madison and Dane County." *Wisconsin Historical Collections* 6 (1872).

Draper, Lyman. *Madison: The Capital of Wisconsin, Its Growth, Progress, Condition, Wants and Capabilities*. Madison, WI: Conklin and Proudfit Printers, 1857.

Durrie, Daniel. *A History of Madison, the Capital of Wisconsin; Including the Four Lake Country*. Madison, WI: Atwood & Culver, 1874.

Eighteenth Census of the United States, 1960: Population. Vol. 1, part 51. Washington, D.C.: United States Bureau of the Census, 1960.

Evjue, William T. *A Fighting Editor*. Madison, WI: Wells Printing Company, 1968.

Fifty Years of Church Work: 1840–1890. Fiftieth Anniversary of the First Congregational Church. Madison, WI, 1890.

Flowers, Frank A. *Annual Report of the Bureau of Labor and Industrial Statistics*. Madison, WI, 1888.

Glad, Paul W. *The History of Wisconsin*. Vol. 4, *The Progressive Era, 1893–1914*. Madison: State Historical Society of Wisconsin, n.d.

Goldsmith, Leslie H. "German-Jewish and Russian-Jewish Immigration: Assimilation and a Ghetto in Madison." *Journal of Historic Madison* 3 (1977).

Hartmann, Susan M. *The Home Front and Beyond: American Women in the 1940s*. New York: MacMillan, 1984.

Hemlin, Richard. "Wisconsin Korean War Stories: Veterans Tell Their Stories from the Forgotten War." *Wisconsin Magazine of History* 91 (Spring 2008).

Hibbard, Benjamin. "The History of Agriculture in Dane County, Wisconsin." *University of Wisconsin Bulletin no. 101, Economics and Political Science Series* 1, no. 2 (n.d.).

Higham, John. *Strangers in the Land: Patterns of American Nativism, 1860–1925.* Brunswick, NJ: Rutgers University Press, 1988.

Hill, Joseph A. *Women in Gainful Occupations, 1870 to 1920*. Washington, D.C.: U.S. Government Printing Office, 1929.

Hurn, Ethel A. *Wisconsin Women in the War Between the States*. Madison, WI, 1911.

International Directory of Company Histories. Vol. 58. N.p.: St. James Press, 2004.

Janik, Erika. "Food Will Win the War." *Wisconsin Magazine of History* 93 (Spring 2010).

Jones, C.E. *Madison: Its Origin, Institutions and Attractions*. Madison, WI: W.J. Park and Company, 1876.

Journal of Historic Madison (1975–present).

Keyes, Elisha W. *History of Dane County*. Madison, WI: Western Historical Association, 1906.

Knapp, J.G. "Early Reminiscences of Madison." *Wisconsin Historical Collections* 6 (1872).

Larsen, Agnes M. *John A. Johnson: An Uncommon American*. Northfield, MN: Norwegian American Historical Association, 1969.

Lawrence, Lee E. "The Wisconsin Ice Trade." *Wisconsin Magazine of History* 48 (Summer 1965).

Leuchter, Sara, and Carole Zellie. *The Third Lake Ridge Historic District: A Walking Tour*. Madison, WI: Madison Landmarks Commission and the Madison Trust for Historic Preservation, 1987.

Levitan, Stuart D. *Madison: The Illustrated Sesquicentennial History.* Vol. 1, *1856–1931*. Madison: University of Wisconsin Press, 2006.

Madison Park and Pleasure Drive Association. *Annual Reports of the Officers of the Madison Park and Pleasure Drive Association*, 1899–1905. State of Wisconsin Collection. Available online at http://digital.library.wisc.edu/1711.dl/WI.ParksDrives.

Madison, Wis. and Its Points of Interest. N.p.: Commercial Pub. Co., 1899.

Merk, Frederick. *Economic History of Wisconsin during the Civil War Decade.* Madison, WI: The Society, 1916.

Moe, Doug. *Surrounded by Reality: The Best of Doug Moe on Madison*. Madison, WI: Jones Books, 2005.

Mollenhoff, David V. "The Capitol and Urban Planning in Madison: 1900–1959." *Historic Madison: Journal of the Four Lakes Region* 25 (1998).

———. *Madison: A History of the Formative Years.* 2nd ed. Madison: University of Wisconsin Press, 2003.

Nolen, John. *Madison: A Model City.* Boston, 1911.

Peck, Rosaline. "Reminiscences of the First House and the First Resident Family of Madison." *Wisconsin Historical Collections* 11 (1888).

Sachse, Nancy C. *A Thousand Ages: The University Arboretum.* Madison, WI: University of Wisconsin Regents, 1965.

Sakrison, David. *Madison (Postcard History).* Chicago: Arcadia, 2009.

Seely, Ron. *Madison & Dane County.* Helena, WI: America & World Geographic, 1993.

Smith, Alice E. *The History of Wisconsin.* Vol. 1, *From Exploration to Statehood.* Madison: State Historical Society of Wisconsin, 1973.

Smith, John Y. "History of Madison." In *Madison City Directory.* Madison, WI, 1866.

State Historical Society of Wisconsin. *Wisconsin Historical Collections.* Vols. 1–21. Madison: State Historical Society of Wisconsin, 1855–1915.

State of Wisconsin. *Private and Local Laws of 1858.* Madison, WI: State Printer, 1859.

Statistics of Madison and Dane County with a Business Directory of the Village of Madison. Madison, WI: Tenney and Carpenter Printers, 1851.

Strand, Roland. *The Story of the* Democrat: *A History of the* Madison Democrat, *a Newspaper Published 1868–1921.* Madison, WI: Webcrafters, Inc., 1948.

Strong, Moses. *History of the Territory of Wisconsin, from 1836 to 1848.* Madison, WI, 1885.

Suckow, B.W. *Madison City Directory.* Madison, WI: Atwood and Rublee Printers, 1866.

Thompson, William F. *The History of Wisconsin.* Vol. 6, *Continuity and Change, 1940–1965.* Madison: State Historical Society of Wisconsin, n.d.

Thwaites, Reuben Gold. *Historical Sketch of the Public Schools of Madison, Wisconsin, 1839–1885.* Madison, WI: Board of Education, 1886.

———. *The Story of Madison.* Madison, WI: University Historical Publishing Company, 1900.

Tripalin, Catherine Murray. *A Taste of Memories from the Old "Bush," 1900–1960.* Madison, WI: Italian-American Woman's Mutual Society, 1988.

U.W. Organizations and Madison Civic Groups. *Earth Week: Lifestyle on Trial, April 17–26*. Madison: Wisconsin Union Public Information Committee, 1970. Available online at www.nelsonearthday.net/collection/422-earthdayinmadison.

Wisconsin Blue Book. Madison, WI: Legislative Reference Bureau, 1962.

"Wisconsin Electronic Reader." University of Wisconsin, Madison Digital Collections. www.library.wisc.edu/etext/WIReader.

Wisconsin State Journal. *Front Page, 1839–1988*. Madison, WI: Wisconsin State Journal, 1988.

———. *Madison 150: A Look at 150 of our Most Influential, Puzzling, Incredible, Scandalous and Quirky People, Places, Controversies, Moments and Things*. Madison: Wisconsin State Journal, 2006.

Women Students' War Work Council. *War Time Recipes*. Madison: Women Students' War Work Council of the University of Wisconsin, 1917.

Youngerman, Henry C. "Theater Buildings in Madison, Wisconsin, 1836–1900." *Wisconsin Magazine of History* 30 (1947).

INDEX

ABOUT THE AUTHOR

Erika Janik is the author of *A Short History of Wisconsin* and *Odd Wisconsin: Amusing, Perplexing, and Unlikely Stories from Wisconsin's Past*. Her work has appeared in *Midwest Living*, *MyMidwest*, *Wisconsin Trails*, the *Wisconsin State Journal*, the *Wisconsin Magazine of History* and the *Onion*. Originally from Redmond, Washington, she now lives in Madison with her husband.